MORE MODERN MYTHMAKERS

25 INTERVIEWS WITH HORROR, FANTASY AND SCIENCE FICTION WRITERS AND FILMMAKERS

MICHAEL MCCARTY

Let the world know:
#IGotMyCLPBook!

Crystal Lake Publishing
www.CrystalLakePub.com

WELCOME
TO ANOTHER

CRYSTAL LAKE PUBLISHING
CREATION

Join today at www.crystallakepub.com & www.patreon.com/CLP

Ever wanted to hang out with legends like Ray Bradbury, Richard Matheson, and Dean Koontz?

TABLE OF CONTENTS

More Modern Mythmakers: Interviews with Horror, Science Fiction and Fantasy Writers and Filmmakers is dedicated the late, great local TV host Chuck Acri of *Acri Creature Feature.*

Also, to the Mythmakers who have since passed away:

From *Modern Mythmakers:*
Forrest J Ackerman
C. Dean Andersson
Ray Bradbury
Dan Curtis
Charlee Jacob
George Clayton Johnson
Jack Ketchum
Herschell Gordon Lewis
Richard Matheson
Joe McKinney
William F. Nolan
Ingrid Pitt
Frederik Pohl

From *More Modern Mythmakers:*
Dennis Etchison
Charles Grant
J.N. Williamson

Also to Joe Mynhardt, in both *Modern Mythmakers* and *More Modern Mythmakers.*
To Kristin DeMarr and Sarah Holderfield for editing the hell out of this book.

And finally to my friends and collaborators Cristopher DeRose, David Kempf, Susan A. Leabhart, Pamela Briggs and Holly Zaldivar who helped me with the lion's share of interviews in this book.

Previously unpublished work:

Steve Alten

Sephera Giron

Owl Goingback

Paul Kane

Ronald Kelly

Jonathan Maberry

Jeff Strand

Bentley Little includes 80% new unpublished material for this book

John Everson includes 60% new unpublished material for this book

Elizabeth Massie includes 50% new unpublished material for this book

Ray Garton includes 40% new material for this book

Nancy Holder includes 40% new material for this book

Larry Niven includes 40% new material for this book

Joe Lansdale includes 40% new material for this book

Alan Dean Foster includes 40% new material for this book

"Foreword" by Jeffrey Thomas

"Afterword" by Gerard Houarner

"Preface" by Michael McCarty

Previously published:

Reggie Bannister (*More Giants of the Genre* by Michael McCarty, 2005)

Terry Brooks (*More Giants of the Genre* by Michael McCarty, 2005)

Charles de Lint (*More Giants of the Genre* by Michael McCarty, 2005)

Dennis Etchison (Horror Garage Magazine 2008, out of print)

Charles Grant (*More Giants of the Genre* by Michael McCarty, 2005)

Jeff Long (*Masters of Imagination* by Michael McCarty, 2010 out of print)

William Stout (*Horror 201,* edited by Joe Mynhardt, 2015)

Harry Turtledove (*More Giants of the Genre* by Michael McCarty, 2005)

J.N. Williamson (*Giants of the Genre* by Michael McCarty, 2003)

Connie Willis (*Modern Mythmakers* by Michael McCarty, 2011, out of print)

Bentley Little included 80% new material for this book (the other 20% previously published in the book *Giants of the Genre* by Michael McCarty, 2003)

John Everson included 60% new material for this book (the other 40% was previously published on the website Masters of Horror UK by David Kempf 2018)

Nancy Holder included 40% new material for this book (the 60% previously published in the book *Masters of Imagination* by Michael McCarty, 2010 out of print)

Alan Dean Foster included 40% new material for this book (the 60% previously published in the books *Esoteria-Land* by Michael McCarty 2010 and *More Giants of the Genre* by Michael McCarty, 2005)

Larry Niven included 40% new material for this book (the 60% previously published in the books *Modern Mythmakers* by Michael McCarty 2008 out of print)

Joe Lansdale included 40% new material for this book (the 60% previously published in the books *Masters of Imagination* by Michael McCarty 2010 out of print)

Elizabeth Massie included 50% new material for this book (the other 50% was previously published on the website Masters of Horror UK by David Kempf 2021)

Ray Garton included 40% new material for this book (the other 60% was previously published on the website Masters of Horror UK by David Kempf and "Cemetery Dance Magazine" by Michael McCarty & Pamela Briggs 2009, out of print)

ACKNOWLEDGMENTS

Welcome back genre fans!

I'd like to thank all twenty five mythmakers for taking time out of their very busy schedules to do the interviews in the first place, and providing whatever assistance and additional material was needed for this book.

Gerard Houarner for writing the introduction, and Jeffrey Thomas for writing the afterword.

Thanks also goes to The Midwest Writing Center, BearManor Media, McFarland & Company, the Rock Island and Davenport libraries, Joan Mauch, AJ, Sarah Holderfield, Jack William Finley, Mel Piff, Terrie Leigh Relf, The Hultings, The Leonards, The McCartys, Chef Steph, The Source Book Store, The Book Rack, Igor's Bistro, The Artsy Bookworm, Amber B, Char, CL Sherwood, Bruce Cook, Brian Kronfeld, Christopher Kowalsky, Jody LaGreca, Camilla, Kimberly Cole Zemke, Marlena Midnite, Blake Powers, *Midnite Mausoleum*, Yeti, and the memories of Latte and Kitty The Bunny.

Finally, I owe a big thanks to Ben Eads, Kristin DeMarr, and Joe Mynhardt of Crystal Lake Publishing for making this book possible. And I'm so blessed to have Cindy McCarty, my beautiful and brilliant wife, who traveled with me on this journey, helping with the difficult task of transcribing, proofreading, going to book signings, and believing in me again.

PREFACE

MY FIRST INTERVIEW was in the 6th grade with my 5th grade teacher Mrs. Stonebraker, who I had the biggest crush on. I started writing for the school newspaper, *The Jaguar News,* in 1973.

Around this same time, I started watching *Acri Creature Feature.* In May of that year, my Uncle Bill Underdonk got married to Audrey (now my Aunt). After their wedding and reception, we were taken home early so my parents could continue the celebration. I talked our babysitter, Jill Manatt (Sexton), into letting us watch the horror TV show that night, which happened to be the movie *Carnival of Souls.*

Acri Creature Feature was a local horror program on WQAD-TV that showed old horror and science fiction movies from the 1950s and 1960s. It was hosted by Chuck Acri who owned a siding company. Acri would try to sell his siding during the breaks, and there would be funny skits featuring groovy ghoulies such as a vampire named Vincent Hedges (a take off on the cigarette Benson & Hedges); a werewolf named Beauregard; Emmit, the hunchback and a caveman.

Each week there was also the "Creep of the Week" contest, where the kids watching the show would send in their drawings for the coveted award. I, of course, entered the contest, failing several times. Then my Mom had an idea.

"Mike, you know you are not a good artist," my Mother said, being very frank and upfront.

"Yeah."

"For months, you've been sending in your drawings and not winning. It's because you aren't very good at art."

Sad, but true, still today.

"If you really want to win, you are going to have to play with your strengths, not your weaknesses," she said.

That made a lot of sense.

"My idea is this. I have this big piece of cardboard. We cover it with aluminum foil and cut up one of your monster magazines and put monster photos on it."

The foil idea confused me and I asked her why put that on it.

"Because Chuck Acri is always trying to push his siding. It is like siding."

I liked the idea a lot . . . but I hated the idea of cutting up an issue of *Famous Monsters of Filmland* and I told her.

Then my Mom really surprised me. "I will give you some money to buy another issue of *Famous Monsters* at Northwest Drug Store."

I went a couple blocks from the drugstore, bought the issue. At the same time, my Mom covered the big piece of cardboard, which was around four feet high by four feet wide. She drew a Big Red Circle in the middle of the cardboard and said, "Leave this blank." Which I did.

I took out several pages of *Famous Monsters* . . . some I would just cut the monster out of the magazine, others, I just took out the complete page and pasted it on.

When I was done, it looked really cool.

My Mom had a full page from the newspaper which had a big photo of Chuck Acri. She cut out that photo and put it in the middle of the cardboard book. And then she told me to write "Our Hero" underneath it. I decided to also have my brother's name on the contest, because he watched the show, and after all, he was my little brother.

My Mom drove over to WQAD and dropped off the monster artwork.

On Nov. 24, 1973, they showed the "Creep of the Week" and you couldn't miss the big, shiny silver cardboard standing in the back, it was blinding. The bad thing, you couldn't really see the monster photos, but it was still cool.

Then Chuck Acri announced the winners and one of them was "Michael and Steve McCarty of Davenport, Iowa."

Our family screamed our heads off. It was awesome! I still have the award on the wall of my office.

Horror hostess Marlena Midnite (who is the longest female horror host in TV history) and producer Blake Powers are continuing the *Acri Creature Feature* tradition on *Midnite Mausoleum.*

But back to writing and interviews . . .

My first professional writing sale was in 1983 for a regional music magazine. My first national sale was in 1993 to *Starlog*. And my first book was in 2003.

I've been doing interviews for a long, long time.

Each interview is like a dance . . . shall we dance again?

This collection of dances, or interviews, started with my first published book, *Giants of The Genre,* 2003. That was followed by *More Giants of The Genre,* 2005. Both were published by Wildside Press, but I left Wildside briefly for about 5 years and started doing interview books for other publishers.

Jonathan Maberry's agent was shopping my book around called *Modern Mythmakers.* I had found a publisher, McFarland & Company, but the late, great Harlan Ellison warned me about the contract so I had the book shopped around by Maberry's literary agent, who was nice enough to do this gratis and on her lunch breaks. After several near misses, the manuscript returned back to McFarland—and they agreed to publish it, but without my agent's representation, which was a major setback for me. The book ended up getting published in 2008. The initial sales of *Modern Mythmakers* was good, so they greenlighted a sequel called *Masters of Imagination.*

Things were stormy with McFarland from the beginning. They basically forced me to sign their contract without agent representation. Then at the last minute, they decided not to publish *Masters of Imagination.*

Harlan Ellison warned me this might happen. I called him again and we had a long talk, but the prospects were grim of McFarland relinquishing the ironclad contract.

I followed my instincts, which I often do in the publishing business, and wrote a long letter to the publisher explaining why I wished they would let me go from the contract. And on my birthday, 2009, they did.

In 2010, I had another publisher, BearManor Media, publish *Masters of Imagination* and a nonfiction book called *Esoteria-Land.* In 2011, BearManor Media published the second edition of *Modern Mythmakers.* Eventually, all three books went out of print.

In 2012, The Amazing Kreskin and I did a nonfiction book of interviews called *Conversations With Kreskin*, which was published by Team Kreskin. The book was featured on national radio and TV, including *Late Night With Jimmy Fallon.* The comedian held up my book in his hands, and pointed it towards the television camera. Like several decades before winning the "Creep of the Week" award, my family screamed our heads off after midnight.

In 2013, Paul Kane, for whom I wrote a great review of his book *Funny Bones* wanted me to write a blurb for his new book called *Sleeper(s)* published by a fairly new company I'd never heard of called Crystal Lake Publishing, out of Africa. I did write a blurb for the book and became really interested in the company and the publisher and editor, Joe Mynardt.

In 2014, I had my essay "Partners In Collaborations" originally published in *Esoteria-Land* republished in *Crystal Lake's Horror 101: The Way Forward.*

I sent Joe my book *Esoteria-Land* to be reprinted by Crystal Lake. He liked the book, but decided to pass because the book wasn't "horror" enough for them. I hit him up with doing a third, mega edition of *Modern Mythmakers*, with the best of the other two editions and some new material. If memory serves me correct, I believe the book ended up being around 120,000 words which was way too long.

Crystal Lake editors and proofreaders, plus a couple editor and proofreader friends of mine, scaled the book back to 90,000 words, and the book was published in 2015.

I guess, I should note, that the ebook edition of *Modern Mythmakers: 35 Interviews With Horror and Science Fiction Writers & Filmmakers* ebook edition had interviews not published in the trade paperback: British writer Kim Newman, the *Dark Shadow* ladies: Kathryn Leigh Scott and Lara Parker, and also Jeffrey Thomas (who wrote the afterword for *More Modern Mythmakers*).

Modern Mythmakers: 35 Interviews With Horror and Science Fiction Writers & Filmmakers was a great seller for Crystal Lake, and I hit Joe up with a sequel idea. He turned it down.

At this point, after doing hundreds of interviews for over four decades, I decided to retire from interviews. The retirement was short lived because I needed content for my monthly blog. So, I continued with doing interviews for my blog.

I hadn't done a nonfiction book for awhile, but when I hit Haunted America up with the idea of doing a true ghost book called *Ghosts of the Quad Cities*, they eagerly agreed. For that book, I had to do several interviews with paranormal investigators, librarians, local historians and others.

Ghosts of the Quad Cities was an Amazon bestseller when the book came out in 2019, and continued to sell very well in 2020 and 2021, still does.

Of course, I did a sequel called *Eerie Quad Cities* in 2021.

I got bitten again by the interview bug. And although it was about five years after the original *Modern Mythmakers: 35 Interviews with Horror and Science Fiction Writers and Filmmakers*, it continued to sell well over the years.

I hit Joe up again and this time he said yes.

When you dance, sometimes you stumble and fall. I had a couple of near misses with interviews. George Romero had a scheduled interview with me, but his manager got Central Standard Time and Mountain Time mixed up and ended up calling me an hour earlier when I wasn't home. When I did get home, I had this message on my voicemail, "Hey, Mike, this is George Romero, are you there?"

I was very excited about interviewing Jennifer Tilly. Her PR guy said I could do the interview on Monday after she came back from being in Las Vegas over the weekend. The problem was, in Vegas she won some celebrity poker tournament and everybody under the sun wanted to interview her.

I came close to interviewing Stephen King (although I did interview his son, Joe Hill once), Richard Laymon, Michael Crichton, Jeffrey Combs, Tom Savini, Ira Levin . . .

I could go on, with other sad near misses of interviews that I didn't get, but it's too painful. I must stop.

On a more upbeat note:

When I was interviewing Ray Bradbury, he said one thing, to this day, I've taken to heart: "The best advice I would give new writers is write what you love."

Thank you, Ray.

Modern Mythmakers and *More Modern Mythmakers* is my love letter to all my fans, friends, families, fellow writers and critics who have all been so incredibly nice to me for almost twenty years of writing books.

One time a fellow writer asked me, "are you sad that you haven't made a million dollars after writing fifty books?"

And I said, "Hell no. I have a million dollars worth of

respect from everybody and that means more to me than any dollar signs do."

The dance is almost finished. I feel very proud that I've interviewed some of the biggest names in the genre for *Modern Mythmakers* and *More Modern Mythmakers*. The music is drawing to a close. Thank you for being a great dance partner through the years, and thank you for supporting my books as well.

Michael McCarty, 2022

FOREWORD:
THE ART OF THE INTERVIEW

GERARD HOUARNER

S O HERE YOU ARE, entering another fascinating journey into the minds of creators of the fantastic, and you might wonder, how did I get here?

You may find yourself in a haunted house, or on another planet, behind the wheel of Pursuit Special, or in a field of zombies, and you might really wonder, how did I get here?

With apologies to the Talking Heads, you got here. Not because of life's random, unconscious choices, but because you are connected, deeply, to the realms of the fantastic.

You're drawn to some, most, or possibly all the flavors, perspectives and tropes of monsters, wonders, horror, heroics, hauntings, discoveries, crimes, and the many other "unusual" imaginative constructions that the human mind creates; sometimes out of nothing, other times out of fear, inspiration, hope, and the close observation of human behavior.

Sometimes it's just easier to wonder, how did I get here?

Let's give Michael props. His job isn't easy.

He's picked the job of not only wondering, how did I get here? (reading and watching movies about these terrible/wonderful places and people), he's also decided to figure out how and why all those terrible/wonderful places and people came to be.

Who are they? Why did they do what they did? Teasing a tiny secret or two from their boiling imaginations, provokes the memory of a detail forgotten in the pressure of creation and the distance of time.

Because once you start to really, deeply wonder about how did I get here? You start asking yourself, how do I find out?

Fortunately, Michael McCarty is here to provide a clue, perhaps a fact or two, or more. At the very least, a context of a reality from which the wonders and terrors emerged to entertain and/or terrorize us.

My perspective on interviews is very different from Michael's. I'm a retired mental health professional. I've interviewed hundreds, perhaps thousands, of people in my 38 years of work: in clinics, and in psychiatric and Forensic hospitals. I've done intake screenings to check for issues and who to assign individuals to, and I've done interviews to find out peoples' histories related to the problems they present and what they want to do about those issues.

In any case, people came to me—sometimes voluntarily, many times as a consequence of behaviors dangerous to themselves and/or others. Their motivation and ability to participate varied depending on their circumstances, health, emotional stability, trust, and desire to return to, or avoid, the community they came from.

Basically, I haven't had to look for people to interview. They come to me.

Michael is another kind of interviewer. Sometimes, I'm sure, people come to him—an agent or rep might seek out interviewers to promote an upcoming release or project. But mostly, from what I've seen and heard from him, he has to hunt them down.

Also, he interviews to discover and share things that may have been secret, or forgotten, about things many people are interested in.

I only interviewed to discover, or help an individual

discover, what might have been secret, or forgotten, and no one, with the possible exception of family or friends (if any were available) might care about.

Not to say that Michael doesn't occasionally use his interviewing skills to massage and encourage self-revelation. But there's no traditional "therapeutic outcome"—though to be truthful, some interviewees are genuinely thrilled by the interaction, and of course relive their own moments of joy and discovery from the past.

But, bottom line, and of course, the media interviewer relationship is different. He may be a part of the publicity campaign for any artistic release. You can catch an interview slot with some hot/new big name, if you have luck, connections, or work for engines of publicity like newspapers, magazines, websites, etc., but you also have to be a hunter. Famous/busy people creating professional work are not seeking out interviewers to chat about this or that past project, or to trade ideas about the current work-in-progress.

Michael is a hunter.

I never fully realized how much work is involved in the art of the interview until I was asked to do this forward, and read some of his interviews a little more closely as well as his own revelations in correspondence, and other people interviewing him.

First off, you have to have a passion for it. You have to love the work. Like creators, you have to be beyond curious—you need to be hungry for the how/why, for the connection with somebody who made something that interested you, had an impact on you, or influenced you, and perhaps even changed your life.

Because you're really going to need that hunger to motivate you as you track down, engage, and make arrangements for interviews. It ain't easy setting up an interview. I had no idea how elusive some folks can be. There's a good amount of detective work that seems to be part of the process. Also, bounty hunting.

I wouldn't go so far as to call it stalking, though.

People are busy. You may be a stranger. People live far away. They may be cranky, or had a bad day. Or the world simply shuts down for a while.

Yes, of course, sometimes you're at a panel, editing your own work while listening to the goings-on, and Neil Gaiman plops down next to you, and you chat and suddenly you've got a great interview with a multimedia creative giant, just like that!

Easy-peasy!

That doesn't happen every day.

You also need the skills. And yes, Michael graduated college with journalism and English majors, and has worked at various media outlets. He's been doing interviews for quite a while, so he was prepared from the outset, and has gained skills and expertise over the years.

Because, just like my mental health interviewees, everyone is different. They may be mad, or in an "altered state," agitated, or low-energy. They may be thinking about all the stuff they have to do, or having trouble remembering something from long ago. They just may not want to be there talking to you right at that moment.

You need to connect to help the interviewee open up. You need to move beyond your own fan-boy awe and wonder, and help the person look inward, remember, connect some dots. Ignite the old passion, and perhaps explore some forgotten corners.

Some of this work is done at the moment, of course. Situational awareness is crucial. Charm helps. It's not easy interviewing people who may not be used to being interviewed, or, conversely, people who have been interviewed a million times and are tired of the same questions. A friend of mine used to complain or get mad about interviewer questions, and sometimes he'd provide them with another, more interesting question.

There's also prep work. Finding questions that will

stimulate memories for the individual, and interest for readers. Digging into the past for old interviews (so you don't ask the same questions) or articles that may have raised interesting details.

All these components of "the interview"—the hunt, skills, engagement, connection, questions and their follow-ups are a lot of work. And then, of course, comes the "clean-up," smoothing out the conversation without changing or omitting anything that was said.

Actually, it tires me out just thinking about it.

I know Michael had to sweat for some of these interviews—exchanging time-differentiated messages on answering machines with a time-zone distant George Romero, or the individual who may or may not get to be interviewed because they suddenly won a big poker event, and, well, other people are getting all the interviews.

However it rolls out, I know the interviews he's already done and the ones he'll finish out with will hit the mark with surprises and special moments, and spark enthusiasm with fans of the people included in this volume.

I know because I've seen how hard he works, and how passionate he is about what he does. He is a master of the Art of the Interview.

Hope you enjoyed the show, and also hope our interviewer will have the energy for another volume down the line.

Because there's always new creators emerging and developing, with wonders and terrors to entertain us, now and in the future.

Gerard Houarner 2022

"My thoughts on the movie, The Meg: *Overall, I loved it. Great cast (I had Jason Statham as my top selection to play Jonas Taylor), amazing special effects and the script stayed with the novel for the most part"*

—Steve Alten

MEG

STEVE ALTEN

STEVE ALTEN GREW UP in Philadelphia, earning his Bachelor's degree in Physical Education at Penn State University, a Master's Degree in Sports Medicine from the University of Delaware, and a Doctorate of Education at Temple University. Struggling to support his family of five, he decided to pen a novel he had been thinking about for years. Working late nights and on weekends, he eventually finished *Meg: A Novel of Deep Terror*. Steve sold his '71 Malibu to pay for editing fees. On September (Friday) the 13th, 1996, Steve lost his general manager job at a wholesale meat plant. Four days later, his agent had a two-book, seven figure deal with Bantam Doubleday. *Meg* would go on to become the book of the 1996 Frankfurt book fair, where it eventually sold to more than twenty countries. *Meg* hit every major best-seller list, including #19 on the *New York Times* list (#7 audio), and became a popular radio series in Japan.

The success of *Meg* and sequels, a prequel and a novella

including; *Meg, The Trench, Meg: Primal Waters, Meg: Hell's Aquarium, Meg: Origins, Meg: Nightstalkers, Meg: Generations and Meg: Angel of Death* and *Meg: Purgatory* (scheduled for publication: summer of 2022) was large in scope.

He also wrote the Loch series: *The Loch, The Loch: Vostok* and *The Loch: Heaven's Lake*, as well as the Dead Bait series: *Dead Bait* (co-written with David Dunwoody) and *Dead Bait 2* (co-written with Ramsey Campbell, who was also interviewed in *Modern Mythmakers: 35 Interviews with Horror and Science Fiction Writers and Filmmakers*).

Other Alten books include: *Sharkman, Undiscovered, Fathom, Goliath, The Shell Game* and *The Omega Project*.

Alten considers *Grim Reaper: End of Days* his best novel. The story, a modern-day *Dante's Inferno,* takes place in New York when a man-made plague strikes Manhattan. And at the age of 47 he was diagnosed with Parkinson's Disease.

Over the years, Steve Alten has been inundated with emails from teens who hated reading . . . until they read his novels. When he learned high school teachers were actually using his books in the classroom (*Meg* had been rated #1 book for reluctant readers) Steve launched Adopt-An-Author, a nationwide non-profit program designed to encourage students to read. Teachers who register for the program (it's free) receive giant shark posters, free curriculum materials, student-author correspondence, an interactive website, and classroom conference calls/visits with the author. To date, over 10,000 teachers have registered, and the success rate in getting teens to read has been unprecedented. For more information click on www.AdoptAnAuthor.com.

For more about the author go to: www.Stevealten.com

MORE MODERN MYTHMAKERS: The *Meg* movie hit the

theaters over two decades after the book was published. Why did it take so long for the novel to hit the silver screen? What were your thoughts on the film? What did you like, what didn't you like?

STEVE ALTEN: The first 100 pages of the manuscript and a treatment were optioned by my literary agent Ken Atchity and his associate Warren Zide to Disney's Hollywood Pictures. Two weak scripts which ignored the novel, Warner Bros. greenlighting of *Deep Blue Sea* and the firing of the head of the studio combined to send the project into turnaround and back to me in 1998. In 2005, my friend Nick Nunziata (creator of *C.H.U.D.*) sent the book to his friend Guillermo del Toro and *Hellboy* producer Lloyd Levin. They had me write a script, then attached Jan de Bont (*Twister*) as director. We polished the script and then the package was optioned to New Line Cinema. NL brought in Shane Salerno to write a new script. The next 2 years were FUBAR. Way too many producers attached, no clear leader split everyone into two factions with two completely different visions and budgets (Shane Salerno wrote a $140 million version of *Moby Dick* with a shark—ignoring the novel) and Toby Emmerich (who never read the novel) wanted a $70 million version of *Open Water*. Thankfully, the project went into turnaround again (I was diagnosed with Parkinsons during that stressful time).

Earlier that year, I had met Belle Avery through a close friend who was interviewing her for his entertainment company which had acquired the pub rights to *Meg* #1 and *The Loch*. Belle loved both novels and she was the only one I trusted, so I fired everyone and optioned both projects to her. We co-wrote a new script which STAYED TRUE TO THE NOVEL. Through hard work, perseverance, and selling her properties and possessions she raised $150 million and brought in Gravity Pics. She took the package to Warner Bros for distribution, and they wanted in.

My thoughts on the movie, *The Meg*: Overall, I loved it. Great cast (I had Jason Statham as my top selection to play Jonas Taylor), amazing special effects, and the script stayed with the novel for the most part. What I didn't like was not being involved as a resource during the process. After 8 novels and 25 years of creating new fresh scenes and doing a thousand hours of research, who really knows more about Megalodons than me? There were a few science errors I would have fixed, and the depths never played a serious part, plus the Meg's tail doesn't move anatomically as it should (watch how my SeaMonsterCove.com F/X director Steve Clarke does it). Still, *The Meg* was an amazing first movie in the series, and I truly believe they will only get better.

MMM: You had to write *Meg: A Novel of Deep Terror* by writing late nights and on weekends. You even had to sell your beloved orange-rust colored 1971 Malibu convertible to help pay for the manuscript's editing fees. What kept you going during those tough times before the book was published?

ALTEN:I believed in the story. Back in 1995-96 most people had never heard of a Megalodon, but sharks were still popular. I also believe in the power of setting goals and never giving up.

MMM: Why did you decide to revise and expand *Meg*?

ALTEN: Because I am a far better writer than I was in 1995.

MMM: I've heard this rumor: Is it true you put advertisements for your books on your car? Does that help with sales?

ALTEN: Does that help with sales? (Laughs). Never . . . Where did you hear that?

MMM: You've written a number of books in the *Meg* series. What was the easiest to write and which one was the hardest to write?

ALTEN: *Angel of Death* is a novella, so that was easiest. *Purgatory* will be the hardest as it will be the last.

MMM: I understand you are a fan of both Peter Benchley's *Jaws* book and Steven Spielberg's movie. My theory why both were a big hit: Chief Martin Brody, oceanographer Matt Hooper, and Captain Quint are the quintessential American characters that everyone loves. And *Jaws* follows the literary tradition of both Herman Melville's *Moby Dick* and Ernest Hemingway's *The Old Man and The Sea,* but with a lot more horror to it. Agree or disagree and what are your thoughts on the book and movie?

ALTEN: For the most part I agree.

MMM: You've written several novel series and stand-alone books. Do the stand-alone works offer you more creative freedom than the series or is it about the same?

ALTEN: The only time I lost creative control was with my first publisher, Bantam/Doubleday. *Meg* was part of a 2 book, 7 figure deal. Arlene Friedman, the president of BDD met with me for lunch in South Florida and told me her goal was to make me the next Peter Benchley. While that's high praise and an amazing goal, it meant all I could write was undersea novels. *Meg*—no problem, but the treatment for novel #2 (which they would name *Fathom*) was about the Mayan Doomsday prophecy which predicted the end of the world on 12-21-12. My editor read through my first 100 pages and sent me an underwater chapter synopsis which had little to do with the Mayan story. We had just moved into our dream house, and everything was riding on me being paid on book two, so I gave them what I thought they wanted . . . leading to two major rewrites in 18 months.

Over the next 30 days, after turning in the rewrite Bantom /Doubleday refused to answer our calls or emails. And then, two weeks before I was to receive $800,000, they canceled the second book with no explanation. But they sure cut the legs out from my career, spinning it in the news, etc. One factor we learned about later was that BDD was being bought out by Bertlesmann and AF was canceling several front-loaded deals to make her accounting look better in order to save her job. She was fired.

We sued to get the rights back (they had advanced money on the second deal). I rewrote the entire *Fathom* novel, and it was published as *Domain*. Later retitled overseas as *The Mayan Testament*, the book has actually outsold *Meg* and was #1 in Spain, Mexico, and Argentina. Unfortunately, the loss of income coupled with Hollywood Pics reversion of MEG led to us losing our dream house, cars . . . and Parkinson's.

MMM: Sorry to hear about having Parkinson's. Has having the disease affected your writing?

ALTEN: PD has affected my typing but not my mind, creativity, or work ethic.

MMM: What is the best advice another writer has given you?

ALTEN: My manager, Ken Atchity, is a writer. He said, "editing a book is like carving up a fish—you chop off the head and the tail and start with the meat in the middle."

MMM: Tell us about your latest project; www.SeaMonsterCove.com

ALTEN: SeaMonsterCove.com is a groundbreaking multimedia entertainment experience where members can interact with the most terrifying sea monsters and prehistoric sharks in history. Over a dozen 360 Virtual Aquarium Experiences. Video games—compete for MEG teeth & other prizes. Two episodic TV series in development, written by me. Download enhanced novels from the Steve Alten library, packed with hundreds of graphic images...and much more! Many thanks to you and my wonderful readers—love you all.

MMM: What was the inspiration for *The Loch*?

ALTEN: My manager suggested it. Initially, I thought it was silly until I spoke to a friend (William MacDonald) who was a cryptozoologist and he told me his theories which made sense . . . many thanks, Bill!

MMM: Last question, if you could be a monster, which monster would you be and why?

ALTEN: I'd be a *Sarcosucchus* (a 47-foot prehistoric croc), crawl out of the Atlantic and plow my way thru this private estate in Palm Beach, then eat the fat orange treasonous swamp rats inside and any other spineless mice lying about, caring only about themselves. Because traitor meat is rancid, I'd probably end up regurgitating everything.

"In Phantasm III, *I stood next to the camera in the mausoleum and we took turns throwing the sphere down the hallway—away from the camera—so we could reverse the direction of the sphere coming into the camera"*
—Reggie Bannister

THE PHANTASM MAN
REGGIE BANNISTER

BY MICHAEL MCCARTY & CRISTOPHER DEROSE

ONG BEACH, CALIFORNIA born Reggie Bannister is best known as the ice cream man extraordinaire in the *Phantasm* series, a role he landed after serving in the Vietnam war and meeting Don Coscarelli, who gave him his first acting gig in Coscarelli's directorial debut, *Jim, The World's Greatest.* Reggie went on to work with Coscarelli in their next pre-*Phantasm* film, *Kenny And Company* before cameras rolled on what would become one of the most memorable (and best) low-budget horror films of all time, *Phantasm*, where he played (fittingly enough) Reg, the guitar-playing ice cream man.

Survival Quest followed, as did the four other *Phantasm* sequels. Reggie, a constant fan favorite at horror cons, has continued his acting in not only television, but other movies like *Silent Night, Deadly Night 4: Initiation,* and *The Wishmaster: Demolitionist,* as well as forming his own production company. Musician, Actor, Screenwriter, and Activist—referred to as "The Hardest Working Man in Horror." His career spans over four decades in television, film, and entertainment with a background that includes writing, acting, and music. As a musician, Reggie has released six musical albums which include rock, country, and folk. He is a veteran of stage and television since the '60s, having played with such groups as Stone Country and Greenwood County Singers.

Besides the *Phantasm* films he was in *Bubba Ho-Tep*, based on a story by Joe R. Lansdale (who is also interviewed in this book), and also stars Ossie Davis and Bruce Campbell. Coscarelli wrote the screenplay and directed the movie.

Reggie's other projects include *Ghastly Love of Johnny X*, *Bonejangles*, *Bloody Bloody Bible Camp*, *Satan Hates You*, *Not Another B Movie*, and *Spring Break Massacre* (with Linnea Quigley, who was interviewed in *Modern Mythmakers: 35 Interviews with Horror and Science Fiction Writers and Filmmakers*).

Reggie's website is: www.reggiebannister.com

MORE MODERN MYTHMAKERS: When you were making the first *Phantasm* movie, did you ever imagine that it would still be popular over four decades later and achieve such cult status?

REGGIE BANNISTER: There are two types of movies that actors secretly or openly want to be involved in. They want to make a really good horror movie and scare the hell out of people, or make a cowboy movie and ride a horse. We got to do a horror movie. When we first did *Phantasm*, it was done with the full intent of making a scary movie. That is what we all wanted to do. I don't think anybody realized that this would still be going on all these years later. Towards the end of *Phantasm*, I had a gut feeling that we had done something pretty special.

MMM: What are some of the changes that you have noticed in independent pictures over the years?

BANNISTER: Special effects. Across the board with the development of technology and artistic techniques. It started, at first, with the special latex for special effects make-up and now we have computer graphics. It's absolutely amazing stuff. The downside to the special effects craze is the story gets lost, good acting gets lost, good concepts get lost to special effects.

MMM: What motivated you to take the role in *Phantasm* in the first place?

BANNISTER: Money (laughs). I'm just kidding. I'm a very creative person and I love to create. Basically we didn't even discuss money, and I really never saw any money until the end of the filming when the picture was picked up. To tell the truth, we all did the movie on spec. I love to act, I love to play music—that is why I did it then and that is why I still do it now. I still throw myself out there to be a part of low budget or almost no budget movies—but my one rule is it has to be a Screen Actors Guild film.

MMM: Do you think the dark humor in the Phantasm series distracted from the horror aspect in the films or not?

BANNISTER: Some people thought that it distracted—some loved the humor. My character Reg—is really a humorless character. He's a musician who has traveled around the world and played guitar with these bands, got tired of it and wanted to settle down in his own little hometown. What does he do? Open an ice cream parlor. He invents his own venue so he can sit there and play guitar and sell ice cream to the kids in an ice cream truck. By the second film, he's thrown into this chaotic nightmare, he's chasing after a Phantasm, characters in a reality that you aren't even sure they exist. When he presents his natural character to these situations, it can be pretty funny at times. It is only funny when it happens to a character who doesn't think it is humorous or doesn't know it is humorous.

If you go back through comedy and you see Harold Lloyd who was hanging from a clock tower, or Charlie Chaplin getting caught in the gears of a modern mechanized society, you never see those characters understand what they are going through is funny; half of it was tragic. They were putting their lives and bodies on the line for a laugh. It was only natural. In the third picture—Reg was sold on the idea of trying to vanquish this evil force in the world, trying to be the soldier, trying to be the heavy-duty warrior type, when in fact he is a musician and an ice cream man (laughs).

For example, there are some people who hate *Phantasm III* because it was humorous, but they still like my character. I talked to other people who loved *Phantasm III* and thought it was their favorite film in the series. It evens out.

MMM: You also appeared in *Silent Night, Deadly Night 4: Initiation* with Maud Adams and Clint Howard (director Ron Howard's brother). How was it being a part of a franchise besides the Phantasm series?

BANNISTER: I'm really good friends with Brian Yuzna (the director of the movie). Brian always wanted to stick me in one of his movies—he got to direct one part of that franchise. It was a lot of fun. What makes the film experience fun is when you're working with professionals. I have worked with other people before where it was a chore just to get a scene shot. That's a drag. But when you work with people like Brian Yuzna or Robert Kurtzman—I was in *Wishmaster: The Demolitionist*—Bob is a real pro. Working on *Silent Night, Deadly Night 4: Initiation*—has to be the longest title in the history of film (laughs). Brian sent me the script, and I was supposed to play the part of an editor of a newspaper called The Public Eye. My character was named Eli, he was a nervous habit guy with a lot of high energy. He smoked constantly. I had a problem with that because I hadn't smoked at the time. I have smoked off and on in my life, but I didn't smoke at that time for about four years. I thought that might be problematic for me having to smoke. I tried to talk to Brian about this the first day of shooting. I said, "Brian, can I talk to you about my character?" He said, "yeah, yeah, sure." "Eli is firing up one cigarette after another." I said "how about this: What if it was sunflower seeds. I keep eating sunflower seeds and stick them inside my mouth and I'm spitting out the seeds everywhere, people could be grossed out. It could be a really funny bit." Brian listened, pulled down on his chin and said, "No Reg, he's a smoker." I said to the assistant director, "Well go get me a couple packs of Marlboro's." I was just hours away from shooting.

Do you know what it's like to smoke when you haven't smoked? You almost pass out, it makes you so high.The very first scene of that film, I got through my lines, I didn't know who the hell I was, or who my character was. And when I watch it back, and know where my head was—during those opening lines—I have to laugh.

MMM: Do you think the smaller budget allowed you greater artistic control?

BANNISTER: Absolutely. That is the joy of independent film. There are a lot of problems with independent films, mostly you don't have the money and you really have to restrain yourself. You have to figure out how to get by without having any money and look like you're putting money on the screen. Talking about special effects, I wish you could have seen us trying to put together some of the special effects for the original *Phantasm*. We still stand beside a camera, with certain scenes with the sphere—the ball flying. In *Phantasm III*, I stood next to the camera in the mausoleum and we took turns throwing the sphere down the hallway—away from the camera—so we could reverse the direction of the sphere coming into the camera. We took turns so we could get the height right for the lens. A long throw so you could see it coming from down the hall. We've done some wacky things to get the effects—it has worked well for us.

MMM: Did *Phantasm II* suffer or benefit from the replacement of Michael Baldwin with James LeGros?

BANNISTER: There was some controversy about that. It is always difficult when you see an original film and you fall in love with it and the characters. Michael was much beloved—obviously—that is why his character has been so much a part of the series throughout (Michael Baldwin was in the original, *Phantasm III: Lord of the Dead, Phantasm 4: The Oblivion, Phantasm 5: Ravager*). When *Phantasm II* came out, there was a controversy among the hardcore fans about the character of Michael and James LeGros. Having said that, James LeGros did a terrific job. I really enjoyed working with James on that film. We had a lot of fun. He's a really great guy and a fine actor. He went on to do *Drugstore Cowboy, Singles,* and *Enemy of the State.*

(Author's note: Director Don Coscarelli personally chose James LeGros over Brad Pitt for the part of Mike in *Phantasm II*).

I can't tell you how many people come up and tell me, "My favorite film was *Phantasm II*." What happened was, with *Phantasm II*, a lot of people who hadn't seen the first one, saw *Phantasm II*. It broke at a time, 1988, when the first film was almost ten years old. There was a whole new generation of people who enjoyed horror films that never saw *Phantasm*. So when they saw *Phantasm II*—it was their initial experience, they had no idea that Michael had been swapped out. They actually had to go back, to see the first one, to find out that character was replaced with another actor. Even the hardcore fans that said "I hate *Phantasm II* because they don't have Michael in it," have come around and done a 360. Irregardless—it is a great film. I have to agree; I think *II* busted out and opened that world of *Phantasm* in a way that had to be done. I think it is a remarkable film for both its special effects and more linear storyline that carries the plot that led to *Phantasm III*, *IV* and *V*.

MMM: Last words?

BANNISTER: The fact that I'm sitting here and talking to you, and know that the readers of *More Modern Mythmakers* want to hear my opinions about horror films and filmmaking is extremely gratifying. I really appreciate everybody's support of my particular job—that's what it is really. I'm an actor; that is my job. To have people appreciate your work is awesome to me. I want to let everyone who has read this particular interview know that I just love and appreciate them for supporting me and my work. I've been involved in some productions that didn't have a lot of money, but had an incredible amount of integrity and wanted really to give everyone the best of conceptual storylines and the best in visuals and acting performances. People like Don Coscarelli, Brian Yuzna, and Bob Kurtzman—they are terrific people and want to do the best for the fans out there. Thank you, thank you—that's my story and I'm sticking with it.

"I use magic sparingly. I use creatures of all kinds sparingly. Because I don't think that's the thing that engages the reader. What I think engages them is characterization and storytelling and a sense of atmosphere"

—Terry Brooks

RUNNING WITH THE DEMON
TERRY BROOKS

BY Cristopher DeRose & Michael McCarty

TERRY BROOKS IS the reigning king of the fantasy field with over 20 *New York Times* best sellers and 25 million books sold worldwide. He grew up in Illinois not far from Sinnissippi Park, which would become his inspiration for creating the Magic Kingdom of Landover series. His vivid imagination as a child began to blossom in high school, where he first began to write stories in the field of speculative fiction. He earned his undergraduate degree at Hamilton College, and a degree from the School of Law at Washington & Lee University.

While practicing law and inspired by the writings of J.R.R. Tolkien, Terry wrote his epic fantasy novel *The Sword of Shannara* in 1977. He quit practicing law and pursued writing full time when he published *Magic Kingdom for Sale-Sold!*

He has written a number of book series' around

Shannara, as well as a book about writing *Sometimes the Magic Works: Lessons from a Writing Life* and two novelizations including *Hook* and *Star Wars: Episode I: The Phantom Menace,* and even a science fiction novel called *Street Freaks. The Shannara Chronicles* premiered on MTV January 5, 2016 and ran for two seasons.

In 2017, Terry Brooks received a Lifetime Achievement Award at the World Fantasy Awards.

MORE MODERN MYTHMAKERS: Your adaptation of *Star Wars: Episode I: The Phantom Menace* was a highly anticipated sequel. Was there any pressure writing that book because the *Star Wars* series was so successful? Was it easy or difficult to work within the framework of a *Star Wars* universe? Did you get any input from George Lucas about the book?

BROOKS: There wasn't any pressure, first of all. I think one of the reasons I was chosen to do this adaptation as opposed to someone else, or someone working in the *Star Wars* world previously, is because I already had established a career and reputation—so it didn't much matter to me one way or another what happened with this project. It was intriguing. It was a great publicity thing. I wasn't in it for the money; I could stand up to George and say, "I don't like what I'm hearing," and walk away. That is the way I went into the project, if I met with him and I didn't like what I heard—I was going to walk away from it. I had such a terrible time doing (an adaptation for) *Hook* years earlier; I was reticent about it.

On the other hand, working with Lucas and the people with Lucas Books was a very enjoyable experience. They were extremely helpful to me—gave me anything I asked for. I went down to meet with them before I started the project and had a couple days at Skywalker Ranch, talking to them, looking at the visuals, and asking questions, reading the script, that kind of stuff and four hours of meeting with George. All of it went so well, I was extremely encouraged and felt they were going to be very supportive—which in fact they were.

George gave me a tremendous amount of leeway in writing that book. He allowed me to change his scenes, he allowed me to change his dialogue, he allowed me to rearrange things. He encouraged me to write original material for the book because his initial idea was to approach the movie from the viewpoint of Anakin Skywalker—the whole *Star Wars* saga is really Anakin Skywalker's story. He couldn't think how to do it visually and make it powerful—it's pretty hard to tell the story from the viewpoint of a boy. George asked me, "How well can you do this with the book?' I told him, "I think I can do it pretty well."

We changed the whole focus, which is why the book doesn't open where the movie opens. It opens with Anakin and stays with him for the duration of the story. We traded ideas.

George liked everything that I did in the end, and he was extremely helpful. It was a great experience. I enjoyed it thoroughly

MMM: You've said you started writing by "copying Tolkien."

TERRY BROOKS: Did I say that? (Laughs). Well, it's not true. I started copying other writers. I've been writing since I was ten years old. I didn't read Tolkien until I was twenty-one or twenty-two. I had lots of other years of trying on other writers' clothing, which I think is fairly typical for young writers starting out. The books they read, by the authors they admire, influence them. They attempt those styles. I wrote a lot of dog and horse stories. I wrote some juvenile mysteries. I wrote a lot of science fiction—which I was enamored of for about two years, in my middle school years. And when I got into high school—I started taking English literature courses—I started trying on a little Thomas Hardy, a little William Faulkner. I wrote the Great White Whale story; I wrote *All Quiet on The Western Front*. I tried on everything you can imagine. I would finish one or two chapters and lose interest. I did a lot of coming-of-age stuff when I went to college, which was really bad (laughs). Nothing worse than when hormones really kick in.

It was all a building process. I was most heavily influenced in form by the European adventure story writers. I wanted to write *The Count of Monte Cristo* and *The Three Musketeers* and *Ivanhoe*—stories like that, but not in a historical context.

When I read Tolkien in my junior and senior year in college *The Lord of The Rings*—there's a format I could find a way to adapt. I set it aside, it was another two years, when I was in a state of insanity, due to being in law school, I had to go back to writing—I picked up where I left off, the idea of using the Tolkien format and began work on *The Sword of Shannara*.

MMM: On the same line, was there a point in your early writing, when you found your own voice, that you knew it wasn't just following a Tolkien format?

BROOKS: In those days, I didn't know anything (laughs). I can say it now because of the time and distance—I don't bruise so easily. I was just trying to get something written. I had finished one book before then, a space opera—a science fiction story and that was it.

I didn't know I could get through an entire book, what was starting out as 300 pages (of *The Sword of Shannara*), I could see that it was going to get bigger than that. It took six years in that course of time. All other things were forgotten, except to get the book written, I wasn't even thinking about, what voice I was using, or how close I was to writing like Tolkien, or whatever, until I was through with the first half, working on the second half of the book—when I did, going back and re-reading everything, it became clear to me I was too close to Tolkien. I really diverted and changed the story in the second half of the book when they discover the Sword of Shannara sword and it's not it. You don't throw out 300 pages after four years of work, so I kept it and figured "I'll go back and fix it later." So, I went on and wrote the second half, and in fact when I got the book accepted, that is what the editor of Del Rey had me do, they said, the first half is too Tolkien-ish to go back and change it—made me re-write most of it.

The more you write, the more time you spend on writing, the more you start to recognize what your voice is, and what it is you have to say, and what it is that is important to you.

MMM: Is there much of a difference between science fiction and fantasy fans?

BROOKS: The most obvious difference is that the fan base for fantasy is much broader. The readership for fantasy is four-to-one than science fiction—maybe larger than that. That is due to the fact that fantasy is a much more accessible form of literature. You don't have to have any pre-existing knowledge to get into a fantasy—you kinda feel that you do with science fiction because it has all that science in there.

There is an off-putting element to science fiction unfortunately, that detours a lot of people from picking it up. Where everybody was raised on fairy tales, legends, and myths and so they can leap on into that.

It is also the reason that mysteries are so popular. It's not because they are all that wonderful—they are so easy to get into. It takes no effort to read one.

MMM: What was the guidebook, The *World of Shannara*

able to tell the readers that the series wasn't? The series has a long history and several characters and settings—is it hard to keep all the facts straight and not contradict anything you have written before?

BROOKS: Yeah, that's one of the reasons I'm glad that someone did that Shannara companion, I can go back and find the answers (laughs). It was somewhat nebulous before, the older I get the tougher it gets for me to remember anything. God knows I go to all these events with the young kids who got the books memorized and they say, "So what do you mean when you did so and so" and I think "Did I do that?" (Laughs). I don't have any memory of it.

It was a companion book to the series; it was conceived by Del Rey—they wanted to do it. I said, "Great—I don't want to write it—get someone else to do it, I'm not interested." I've never been interested in peripheral stuff of any kind. I'm only interested in the books.

So, they hired Teresa Patterson, a fan of the work and she did a terrific job of researching everything. I spent several days with her and David Cheery (the artist for the book) both talking about the way the (Shannara's) world works. And Teresa would say, "What do you mean by–" "What was your intention," "What do you think happened?" and in a lot of incidents I said, "Beats me. What do you think?" And she would go back and write it. They did a really great job with it. A lot of the book is Teresa's invention about what she thinks are the connections, and what would happen and so forth, and all of it is David's visuals. All I did was edit and oversee the whole thing, then fill in "the blanks"—it was not a project I was enamored of undertaking.

MMM: In the first three *Shannara* novels, the books were more separate stories with recurring characters. The following five were more of a continuing series. Was this a shift in direction or something you planned?

BROOKS: The first three *Shannara* novels were written while I was still practicing law. Each took a number of years to write. *Sword* took six or seven all together. *Elfsongs* took almost three. That was after a misstep on what was going to be the second book, so there was a five-year gap between book one and book two. The next one, *Wishsong*, took another two or three years to write—there were big gaps of time in there, when I wasn't a full-time writer.

After I wrote *Magic Kingdom* and quit being a lawyer and became a full-time writer, I began to look at the writing in a different way. I still wanted to do the epic fantasy stories in conjunction with *Shannara*. When I sat down to work out *Heritage*, which turned out to be a four-book set, I envisioned it as a trilogy. I'm always looking to do something different, as before I used single books with one Shannara character and in the last book two, I decided I was going to write about a whole family and follow them through a set of books that would have a continuing storyline, that would have smaller storylines that would wrap up within. It was quite ambitious, but something different.

When I began to map *Heritage* out, it became clear that it would have to be four books. That's what it ended up being.

Then I was sick of Shannara again, which happens periodically, then I went off with the *Magic Kingdom of Landover* series for a couple of years. Then I was going to do another book in the series, but my editor said, "No, we need you to do another Shannara book first." And that is when I decided to respond to all the requests from fans for answers to what happened before *Sword* in various ways; that is, where the First *King (of Shannara)* came from, which is a separate story altogether.

Now I'm back doing a whole different thing. I'm writing two trilogies that piggyback off each other. *The Voyage of*

The Jerle Shannara is a set of three books, and 20 years after that you'll get into a new set—which will use some of the themes and storylines started in the first one and a couple of the characters.

I don't like writing about the same characters over and over again. To me, it's more interesting to change the characters, but at the same time also to change the format, so that's what I have been pretty much doing.

MMM: What is your favorite book in the *Shannara* series?

BROOKS: I don't think I can answer that question, and the reason I couldn't is because each of them means something different for me. Obviously, *Sword* was a breakthrough book—you have to say that was important to me: the book that really made my career. But *Elfstones* was a tremendous accomplishment because I came back out of the ashes of a book that was thrown away to write that book. It was an extremely strong book. You can go on from there and talk about each of the other ones—it's really hard to choose.

The answer I usually give, which is probably true, is that my favorite book is the one I'm writing right now. To me, it's the process that matters. I really love the writing process. It's what intrigues me; it's what keeps me fascinated and going. When the book is done, it's done—it doesn't belong to me anymore. It belongs to the readers.

MMM: *Running with the Demon* had the power of small-town children's point of view of magic. Is that easier or harder to write when you're an adult?

BROOKS: I think it is much easier. I think the most important thing you have as an adult is, and you don't have from back then, is perspective. When you're in the moment, you don't have the same appreciation for what is going on. I think about all the stuff that happened when I was a kid.

It didn't mean the same thing to me then because I didn't have perspective on it.

Now of course, you can look back and see a lot of stuff. You get a better sense of what is important, what those things meant, or what they do mean in the larger sense.

What it means to grow up in a small town. What it means to believe in magic as a buyable concept because you believe anything is possible. We lose all that along the way. We lost a lot of it unfortunately and it is hard to get back.

MMM: In fantasy, it is better to have limits on the power of magic. Do you agree or disagree with that?

BROOKS: I agree. I'm a huge advocate that less is more. I use magic sparingly. I use creatures of all kinds sparingly because I don't think that's the thing that engages the reader. What I think engages them is characterization, and storytelling, and a sense of atmosphere.

It's like that with *Signs*. They have been comparing it to (Alfred) Hitchcock. What is so great about Hitchcock and his filmmaking is that he never showed you a whole lot of anything; he just suggested the presence of it. It was the suspense that made his movies so great. You were always on the edge waiting for the next thing to happen. You never really saw anything, maybe once or twice something overt happened and you weren't exactly sure. I think there's a lot to be said about that in your storytelling, too. You want to be careful of not overdoing it. You don't want to get into a place where magic is solving all your problems. That's poor storytelling.

Not only should magic be used sparingly, but also it should have deep significance when you do it. I can't read fantasy where magic is commonplace and thrown out there at the drop of a hat. I'm supposed to accept it's how it is in that world. I think, oh well, who cares? I want to know about the people. The magic on the people when they use it. Those are the things that interest me.

It's like presidents. Presidents go into office one person and come out another. What happens to them? They have all this power, and they use it, and it changes them in different ways. We've seen it time and time again.

These corporate CEOs, did they grow up little bastards? (Laughs). They turned into greedy little bastards when they were in office, when they were in their positions of power with these corporations when they thought they could do anything. That's what's intriguing to me.

MMM: What are your thoughts on your nonfiction book *Sometimes the Magic Works: Lessons from A Writing Life.*

BROOKS: It's a small book on what I learned about being a writer from the past 25 years. Things that happened to me, what they taught me about, about the craft of writing, and what I think is important for writers to know; what they need to do, and that kind of stuff.

MMM: Was *The Magic Kingdom of Landover* a fun series to write? What was your inspiration for Abernathy, the talking dog court scribe?

BROOKS: Yeah, *Magic Kingdom* was a fun series to write. I wrote it looking to write something lighter and a little less dark than the Shannara stories.

Abernathy, well Abernathy was real. Abernathy was a real dog and before I started writing it, he was my dog. When I was working in the library he would come in there and lie down next to me and periodically sleep. He was a soft-coated Wheaten Terrier. In fact, when we did the book, I sent Judy Lynn (editor of Del Rey) a picture of him to show her that he was real, and they had the artist's rendering of the dog on the cover.

Anyway, he would lie there, and he would open one eye and look up at me and I was working on the Shannara books at that time, and one day I looked at that dog and thought, "You know that dog doesn't do one damn thing but lie there all day and look at me." You'd think he could contribute in some way, and I took that thought with me. I thought, "By golly what if that dog actually could do something?"

Then it mushroomed out from there, and I thought well this is his story, and I began to develop Abernathy as a character. It's funny too because I get letters from soft-coated Wheaten Terrier societies and pet owners who all identify with Abernathy the talking dog.

MMM: Do you consider fantasy authors such as Robert Jordan, Terry Goodkind, Charles de Lint, Terry Pratchett, and J.K. Rowling as your contemporaries or competition?

BROOKS: I have no competition (laughs). I don't look at writing as competitive, but as more of an embracing experience for the people involved in it. I don't think we compete against each other actually.

It's not like potential readers say, "I have $25.00, which of these authors am I going to spend my money on?" (Laughs). They go buy that book and that's their book for the year.

The fact is, they will buy as many books as we can put out, if they like our work. The problem is, not any of us can write fast enough.

I don't believe in awards and recognition for work done. I think as a writer, you have an obligation to be the best that you can. I don't think you should be rewarded for doing your job. I don't think we should be choosing one writer over another. I think we all do the best job that we can. We all work hard. It shouldn't be set up as artificial competition.

We all have people whose work we particularly admire, and we all have books that we particularly detest (laughs). That's just the nature of the beast. As a reader we have those prejudices too.

MMM: Last words?

BROOKS: I'll throw in a couple last words. For writers the competition is with other forms of entertainment. It is much easier for a potential young reader to sit down and play a video game, to watch a video or DVD, or go to the movies or listen to music, than it is to read a book. Maybe not so rewarding, however, the trick is finding ways to engage young readers with books.

I think that is the struggle that teachers and librarians and parents and the readers themselves have been going through for a long time.

We need to encourage reading at all levels.

"There are certain tropes in science fiction, fantasy and horror—if you work in the field, you are going to want to write them all. You're going to want to do a werewolf story, a vampire story, a Frankenstein story, time travel, an invisible man, a body-swapping kind of story."

—Charles de Lint

SOMEPLACE TO BE FLYING
CHARLES DE LINT

BY MICHAEL MCCARTY AND SUSAN A. LEABHART

SCIENCE FICTION WRITER Orson Scott Card once said, "There is no better writer now than Charles de Lint at bringing out the magic in contemporary life. The best of the post-Stephen King contemporary fantasists, the one with the clearest vision of the possibilities of magic in a modern setting."

Charles de Lint is widely credited as having pioneered the contemporary urban fantasy genre, contemporary magical realism, and mystic fiction with over eighty published books to date. It is easy to see why he is established as one of the leading fantasy writers in North America.

His novels, novellas, collections, countless short stories, and poems include such books as *Juniper Wiles*, *The Blue Girl*, *The Onion Girl*, *The Wind in His Heart*, *Paperjacks*,

Ghosts of Wind and Shade, The Dreaming Place, Someplace to be Flying, Jack the Giant Killer, Trader, and many more.

De Lint has won several awards, including getting inducted into the Canadian Science Fiction and Fantasy Association Hall of Fame, the World Fantasy Award, Aurora Award, Canadian SF/Fantasy Award, the Prix Ozone, Best Foreign Fantasy Short Story, New York Public Library's Best Books for the Teen Age, HOMER, YALSA, and the William L. Crawford Award. He served as Vice President of the Horror Writers Associations from 1992-1994.

His "The Sacred Fire" was used on the Showtime TV series *The Hunger.*

On top of all of that, he has been the primary book reviewer for *The Magazine Of Fantasy & Science Fiction* since 1987.

He was born in the Netherlands, and is now a citizen of Canada. He is also a musician who specializes in traditional and contemporary Celtic and roots music with his musical partner and wife MaryAnn Harris.

MORE MODERN MYTHMAKERS: You and your Tor editor Terri Windling came up with the term mystic fiction to describe your work. What is it about mystic fiction that makes it a good genre for your writing?

CHARLES de LINT: Mystic fiction is fiction that has elements and roots of folktale and myth in it, but it is strictly fiction. It encompasses historical, rural, urban—whatever kind of thing you are dealing with, as long as it has a myth underpinning.

I like telling stories with people, but also, I've always been interested in stories which are slightly off-filter—I like to put that in a story. It's interesting. There are a lot of books that are published in mainstream or films and things like that would be considered fantasy material except it isn't marketed that way. It is all a marketing thing. In fiction, Alice Hoffman, for instance, has little mysterious goings-on like witches or ghosts in her stories, but no one ever considers them to be fantasy.

In movies like Tom Hanks' *Big* or *Splash*, and John Travolta in *Michael* or *Phenomenon*, *City of Angels* or *Pleasantville*. They are all fantasy films.

I'm intrigued by ordinary, real people in their lives and how things go on. I also like something else in the mix that makes it more than just the world around me and makes it more fun to write about.

MMM: *Forests of the Hearts* features The Gentry. Is The Gentry based on real folklore, or something you created?

De LINT: They are kind of a mix of the old Sidhe—who are these tall dark elves of Ireland, as opposed to the ones that end up in Victorian children's books. In folklore, the elf races were quite immoral. They were very dangerous—they weren't kindly flower fairies and it's a play on that.

It is also a play on the hard men you see in bars and pubs. They are just nursing these long standing grievances—you'll find them in Irish bars; you'll find them in any kind of bar. They are the brooding person in the corner. The reason I dealt with the Irish in that book . . . I wanted to deal with that aspect of the drinking. The Irish stereotypes aren't real, but unfortunately, there are going to be people who embrace them anyway.

That wasn't the main thrust of the book, to be honest with you. That is like one little part of it. The main thrust of the book was the idea of home—where it is and what it means to you.

MMM: How do you keep the place of Newford (an imaginary place in his Newford series) fresh for you to keep writing about that setting?

De Lint: I have no idea. I enjoy writing about the place—and revisiting the characters. I have been dealing with the same core of characters in the novels, and I'm going to stop doing that very soon. I prefer to have a new cast of characters for every novel. I'll probably still use those guys for short stories or background stuff.

Newford is just an amalgam of all the different cities I have seen. That is where the place came from. If I go to a city that has something really cool—I'll just put it into a Newford story.

MMM: Is the main theme of *Trader* about identity?

De Lint: Yes.

MMM: With all the body-swapping that goes on in *Trader*, was it hard to keep the characters straight when you have them in different bodies?

De Lint: I think it is easier to do body-swapping in fiction than in film. In film, the actor is going to have to develop all the mannerisms of the other character. But in your writing, you stick with the same characteristics for the character. It doesn't matter what body they are in, you just stick with the way their mind works. I didn't have any trouble with that at all.

There are certain tropes in science fiction, fantasy and horror—if you work in the field, you are going to want to write them all. You're going to want to do a werewolf story, a vampire story, a Frankenstein story, time travel, an invisible man, a body-swapping kind of story. These are the things that intrigue you about the field in the first place—so you're going to want to try to see how you do it as well. I wanted to try that kind of story for the fun of it. I didn't think it was original—I just wanted to see what I could do with it.

MMM: I liked *Trader* a lot and would highly recommend it. It was in the same vein as Anne Rice's *Tale Of The Body Thief*, but you had a lot of fun with this tale and it shows with the writing.

De Lint: Thank you. One of the things that writers talk about a lot is that there are ten plots that they keep reusing. I think there is a certain validity to that. What we do as writers . . . It's not the plot or the ideas that make a book stand out—it is what you, as an individual, bring to it. As long as you can write honestly and effectively, I think readers will appreciate that. If you give ten writers the same plot, you'll have ten different stories.

MMM: Can you share some of your experiences working with artist Charles Vess on *Medicine Road?*

De Lint: I've done a previous book with Charles Vess for Subterranean Press called *Seven Wild Sisters*. Our editor/publisher Bill Schaffer was really happy with the way it was done. He wanted three more books that were connected. So we decided to connect them to the seven wild sisters and follow some of the sisters in each book.

With *Medicine Road*, Charles and I decided we wanted it to be set in Arizona because he wanted to draw desert scenes and I wanted to write about them. We took the road trip the character took and I came home and wrote the book.

Charles had lots of reference material and took lots of photographs. He had actually been to all the places. It was easy to write about and easy for him to draw.

It was a very fun project—we enjoyed doing it. I don't know when in our schedules we can open it up enough to do another one, but down the road we certainly hope to.

MMM: You are also a book critic for *The Magazine of Fantasy & Science Fiction*. As an author, do you feel you have a little more insight than most critics might? Also, how many books do you receive in a given year?

De Lint: I have no idea how many books I get (laughs)—but I can only review three a month. I don't consider myself a critic, I consider myself a reviewer—there is a big difference. Basically, what I try to do with my column is sit down with the readers and talk about books we like and why we like them.

I think I've only given one completely negative review I've done so far. I don't feel like reading bad books. Therefore, if the book is bad, I don't finish it. I have so little space in my column. I prefer to concentrate on the good books and point them out to the people who might not have had a chance to read or notice them.

I have certain sympathy for authors. I probably don't come down as hard on them as a person who doesn't write might. I know how much work they put into it, to start with. I also know that just because I don't get it, it doesn't mean it's not there. There are lots of times when I write things which will seem absolutely crystal-clear. My editor or MaryAnn, who is the first editor, will not get it, and it baffles me. It's not because they are stupid—it's a matter of miscommunication. Sometimes that will happen. I will point those miscommunications out to authors, but I don't feel it is my job to come down hard on people because of it.

MMM: You have written books for adults and young adult readers. Do you have to write in a different mindset for these two different audiences?

DE LINT:I don't really write them differently. The only thing I do differently is make sure there is no swearing in them, and try to tone down any violent or sexual content.

On the other hand, I'm getting readers who are eleven or twelve who liked *The Little Country* (laughs). Those same kids are reading Stephen King. Younger readers who are reading above themselves, of what we consider they should be reading—they have been doing that for years. I don't think it is right to write down to anybody.

MMM: In your novel, *Someplace to be Flying*, the Crow Girls are fascinating creatures. What was your inspiration for them?

De LINT: I have no idea. Probably just watching crows. (Laughs). I just moved a year ago and my new neighbor told me: "Until you moved in that house, we didn't have crows in the neighborhood." (Laughs) I love watching crows, they are so smart and so clever—they are goofy but they are quite serious.

Most people don't like crows. I'm quite delighted by the fact that I've been getting a fair amount of mail from people saying stuff like: "I've always hated crows, but after reading your book, I look at them in a different light and they make me smile."

MMM: The trickster plays a major part in several of your novels. Why are you drawn to this character?

De LINT: I'm drawn to outsiders, people who are out of the regular society like artists, people in the creative endeavors, and criminals. The trickster is also fun. There is one level where he/she is very clever where they can get out of predicaments and they get into predicaments as well. They make for a fascinating character.

MMM: Regarding *The Onion Girl*—there is a strong thread of redemption running throughout the book. How did you arrive at the concept?

De LINT: I've known for years that I'd be writing a story about Jilly, but knowing her backstory, I put it off for a long time. I like her too much to put her through what she must go through in this book. But you can't put things off indefinitely, and the basic premise behind the book has stayed strong in me over the years—how the same traumatic event could so differently affect people who have come up out of the same environment—so much so that I finally had to write about it.

MMM: Given the chance, would you stir the Raven's Pot?

De LINT: Probably (laughs). I know I shouldn't do it, I probably would.

MMM: Last words?

De LINT: It's a hard world out there and we should all take care of each other. That's all.

"For The Fog (novelization) I worked very closely with John Carpenter and company. They were in post-production of the film and it was near where I lived. I arranged to go there to meet with them and view the reels of film that they were cutting—I saw a lot of material that wasn't in the finished film"

—Dennis Etchison

TALKING IN THE DARK
DENNIS ETCHISON

PETER STRAUB CALLED Dennis Etchison "one of horror's most exciting, most radical and innovative talents." The late, great George Clayton Johnson called him, "One of the greatest living writers of psychological horror," and the late, great Charles Grant called him "the best short story writer in the field today, bar none. " Some of Etchison's highly praised works include such novels and short story collections as *Darkside, The Dark Country, The Death Artist, California Gothic, Double Edge, Shadow Man, The Blood Kiss,* and *Talking in the Dark.*

The California writer started writing short horror fiction in the early 1960s, and hasn't stopped since. Highly respected for being an editor as well as an author, he has edited numerous short story collections and anthologies.

He has won the British Fantasy and World Fantasy

Awards and received the Lifetime Achievement Award from the Bram Stokers in 2016.

Dennis Etchison passed away on May 28, 2019.

MORE MODERN MYTHMAKERS: Why do you write horror?

DENNIS ETCHISON: It's easy to give a glib answer to a question like that, "I can't write anything else." But the truth of the matter is, I never set out to be a horror writer. I never thought of my stuff as horror—I was writing the kind of story I thought would be good, and then I went about to sell it. As the years went by, I was selling more in the horror field.

During the '70s I had been selling science fiction, but things started to really get going for me in horror. I don't mind it, but it was by no particular design. I'm writing the kind of story that reflects what I see, think and feel when I look out the window here. I don't think, "What are the elements of a horror story? And how should I go about writing it?"

MMM:When you started out writing, you were writing science fiction for such magazines as *The Magazine Of Science Fiction And Fantasy*, and *Orbit*. Was there any reason that you particularly wanted to get out of science fiction or were you more comfortable writing horror?

ETCHISON: I think it's just the way that your mind develops over the years. I had been a lifelong science fiction fan, loved it, and had some familiarity with horror. I was a fan of horror movies and certain frightening stories that I'd read like "An Occurrence On Owl Creek Bridge" by Ambrose Bierce.

I just found that after the so-called "new wave" movement in science fiction, which was in the late '60s early

'70s, there seemed to be a reaction against that. Science fiction seemed more conservative or right-wing both in its politics and its literary techniques, and at the same time there opened a renaissance in the horror field. It was started by the small press magazines like *Whispers,* and eventually the success of *Rosemary's Baby* and *The Exorcist.*

Then there was Stephen King, and there came to be a renaissance in horror. More editors were interested in looking at horror than the science fiction editors. The remaining science fiction editors seemed to be fairly conservative and traditional in their standards, so I found greater acceptance among horror, so-called, dark fantasy editors.

You know when you finish a story, you go down the list of places to send it, and when it comes back you send it out to the next place on the list, and it seemed that I was getting more acceptances in the horror field and then also, as I said before, I think your personality, your view of the world changes, as time passes. I just began to see my point of view reflected in the horror field more than in the science fiction field.

MMM: Early in your career, do you get your start in men's magazines?

ETCHISON: Yes. My first short story sale was published in a men's magazine called *Escapades* when I was still in high school. I'll never forget going down to the little store near my folk's house to buy a copy when it came out. They didn't want to sell it to me; it was a nudie magazine with naked women in it. I showed them that I was in the magazine and they finally sold me a copy.

I didn't set out to be just a science fiction writer, or any particular kind of writer. So, I would purposely try to sell a story to a slick magazine, a genre magazine, and a mainstream magazine. I would attempt to alternate one after another; every third one would be one of those, so I wouldn't get typecast. It turned out that I would get typecast, I'm only known as a horror writer now. That is partly because the other markets had dried up.

MMM: Another early magazine you were published in was the men's magazine *Cavalier*. That magazine also launched the careers of Stephen King, Mort Castle, and Bentley Little. What kind of short stories did you write for them?

ETCHISON: It turned out that one of the editors at *Cavalier* was Douglas Allen, who had been the editor at *Escapades*. Writers sent them because they paid better than the science fiction magazines did. I sold them a horror story and a science fiction story—after they were rejected by the science fiction and horror magazines. Unfortunately, no one saw them (laughs). I don't know who was reading *Cavalier* at that time. It was one of the magazines that were following in the wake of *Playboy*. For a few years there were a whole bunch of slick, would-be sophisticated magazines in the mold of *Playboy*. *Cavalier* in the early'70s was the best of the lot.

They paid a little bit more, not as much as you think—about what one could get for a short story today. There has been no increase to account for inflation. Economically, it was suicidal to continue to write short stories because they pay essentially what they paid when I started.

I knew that Steve King had stories in *Cavalier*, I talked to him once about that, we compared prices of what we got for our stories. We were both aware of each other's stories, but we weren't in the same issues.

MMM: Talking about short stories, one of my favorite stories you wrote is "The Late Shift," in which a man discovers the local 7-Eleven is staffed by zombies. What was the inspiration for this terrific tale?

ETCHISON: I was riding in a car with a couple of friends. We saw someone walk in front of us at a stoplight that had that shambling walk that a half-dead person might have. I made some remark about "That is really a dead person and they just keep the person going through medical means." Within thirty seconds of laughing and talking, I had explained the whole story.

They take these people and they inject them with some kind of "Super Adrenaline" right in the heart muscle so they can get an extra couple of days of work out of them after they die. Afterwards, after I thought about it—the theme seemed clear—it was an anti-capitalist story. The idea was how the capitalist system can extract its pound of flesh from you in labor even after you die. There is that mysterious period of time, two or three days between the time you died and the time that you're cremated or buried. In a true capitalist system, which is interested in utilizing its resources to the max, they might find a way to make money off of you during that time, before your body is planted in the ground.

MMM: You did novelizations of such books as *The Fog*, *Halloween 2*, *Halloween 3*, and *Videodrome*. Did you get a chance to meet John Carpenter or David Cronenberg. And if so, what were they like?

ETCHISON: The main reason I took those assignments was because I was a fan of theirs and I wanted to be able to meet them. For *The Fog*, I worked very closely with (John) Carpenter and company. They were in post-production of the film and it was near where I lived. I arranged to go there to meet with them and view the reels of film that they were cutting—I saw a lot of material that wasn't in the finished film. There is material in *The Fog* novelization that is shot, but not in the final film, there are words which were on the final soundtrack that were indecipherable in the release prints. I worked with the soundman on the film. Who played me back the words that were being spoken, separated from the other sound, so I could hear what was actually being said. I tried to duplicate the color scheme, the visual style, the camera movements, everything about *The Fog*, so the book would be a true reflection of Carpenter's style and attitude. I had the benefit of asking him questions of what he was getting at in a particular scene. In a sense, the book is a sort of an expansion of the film, rather than just a rip off of it.

The same thing with David Cronenberg. I really didn't want to do another novelization at that point. I absolutely adored Cronenberg's work. I had a chance to go to Toronto, where he was editing *Videodrome,* and I got four different drafts of the script. I saw footage that had been shot and not used. I saw a reel that was edited in a different order. I was able to talk to the director at some length at the studio and at his home about the film. I very much enjoyed that. I will always be grateful that it allowed me to meet Cronenberg— a wonderful artist, and someone who I feel close to artistically.

MMM: Last question, what is your favorite, most perfect Dennis Etchison book or short story? And why?

ETCHISON: The one that hasn't been written yet. I have never written something that I felt hit the target 100%. Each time I try to get a little closer to the center of the target. I have yet to score anything that I would consider first rate. Some of them are closer to what I had in mind than others.

When I look them over, I would say that *The Dog Park* isn't bad, *The Detailer* isn't bad, *Red Dog Down* isn't bad. *Inside The Cackle Factory* and *The Dead Cop* aren't bad, but that is because they are more recent and to where I am now, but probably ten years from now I'll be appalled.

When I was putting together my 40 year retro collection for Stealth Press called *Talking in the Dark*, I had to look through all my stories and the ones I had tentatively listed to be in the book were often a great disappointment when I re-read them. Sometimes I thought they were appalling; they were poorly written. They are not as you remember them because you are more sophisticated now than you were then. Your standards keep on improving; your ability keeps improving.

"I write supernatural, erotic horror. Basically stories with demons, ghosts and dark magic, that tend to have sexual content. Because, well . . . you have to keep it interesting!"
—John Everson

VOODOO HEART
JOHN EVERSON

BY DAVID KEMPF & MICHAEL MCCARTY

JOHN EVERSON IS a Bram Stoker Award-winning horror author with more than 100 published short stories and 12 novels including *NightWhere, The Devil's Equinox, Siren, The Pumpkin Man, The Family Tree, The House by the Cemetery, Violet Eyes,* and *Voodoo Heart.*

Everson grew up in Tinley Park, Illinois, a suburb of Chicago. After graduating from the University of Illinois with a degree in Journalism, he landed a job with *The Star Newspaper* in Chicago Heights, IL, where he began the weekly music review column "Pop Stops." He wrote this column for the newspaper for nearly 20 years, even after leaving *The Star* as a full-time reporter to serve as an editor for the *Illinois Entertainer* magazine for four years. His first two novels feature a reporter, Joe Kieran, as the lead character, drawing on his experience from his journalism background.

His first novel, *Covenant* won the Bram Stoker Award

for a First Novel in 2005. His characters Danika and Mila Dubov appear in the Netflix series *V Wars*.

Everson lives with his wife, Geri, and son, Shaun, in Naperville, Illinois.

For information on his fiction, art, and music, poke around on his website: John Everson: Dark Arts at www.johneverson.com.

He is also on Facebook at www.facebook.com/johneverson and on Twitter at www.twitter.com/johneverson.

MORE MODERN MYTHMAKERS: What was the inspiration for *Voodoo Heart* and how do you feel about comparison to the movie and book of *Angel Heart*?

JOHN EVERSON: The inspiration for *Voodoo Heart* came more than 20 years ago when I visited New Orleans for the first time in the late '90s. It was pre-Katrina, and I was there for a solid week for a convention my day job was running. I didn't get out during the days much because I was working, but I absolutely loved the city as much as I could see of it at night—the heat, the food, the music . . . the French Quarter, the old mansion district . . . I took a streetcar one day and sought out Anne Rice's house. I remember having to rush back from walking the Garden District because I was late for a business dinner. Hated to strap on a tie and suit jacket after exploring in shorts and sandals!

Anyway . . . after that trip, I wrote a story called "Vigilantes of Love" as the "title track" for my second short fiction collection, and the story was set in New Orleans and focused on the impact of a voodoo curse on a jaded detective named Ribaud. My editor at the time said it should be a longer story, and while I didn't think so at the time, a decade later I outlined an idea for expanding the story and submitted it to Leisure Books. It wasn't chosen from my stack of story outlines at the time (I wrote *Siren* or *The*

Pumpkin Man instead) but a few years later, while I was sitting in a bar in New Orleans while there for another business meeting, I decided I would finally write it—almost 20 years after I wrote the original short story.

As far as comparisons to *Angel Heart*, I honestly don't know. I haven't read the book, and I saw the movie in the theater over 30 years ago when it first came out in the late '80s and haven't seen it since. So, all I remember about it is that it had to do with voodoo and Lisa Bonet got in trouble with her Cosby sitcom career because of the raciness.

MMM: *Voodoo Heart* is set in New Orleans. What places are real and which places are made up in the books?

EVERSON: Most of the places are invented but influenced. I've been there several times since that first trip that inspired the "Vigilantes of Love" short story. There are specific places I love that are settings—every time I'm in New Orleans I eat at Redfish Grill, so that gets a cameo. And I have written chapters of books and sections of short stories while sitting at Turtle Bay bar on Decatur. I actually decided to write this book while sitting there one night so, that gets plugged a couple of times. But most of the "locations" are "influenced" by my visits to New Orleans— amalgams of places I have seen—more than being exact descriptions of specific spots in the city.

MMM: *Siren* was the last book Leisure horror line published. Does anyone say, "Hey John, you killed Leisure books?"

EVERSON: Ha . . . I say it. Because I did it *twice*. August of 2010 was when *Siren* was released, in tandem with Brian Keene's *A Gathering of Crows*. A couple weeks later, it was announced that Leisure was going to not publish anything else for several months while they retooled. They relaunched a trade paperback format horror line the following year under the parent company imprint, Dorchester Books. So, in June of 2011, they reissued *Siren* in Trade Paperback. I was psyched to see it back on the shelves at Borders Books that summer, but a few weeks later, Borders announced bankruptcy, so that was a short-lived victory. And then that October, Dorchester Books released my fifth novel, *The Pumpkin Man* in trade paperback, and that, I believe, was the last original non-reprint fiction they released—within a few weeks, Dorchester canceled all future releases and went into bankruptcy themselves, eventually selling all of their catalog to Amazon's 47North Books (where my first five novels remain).

So yeah, I guess I killed them twice!

MMM: What got you interested in the Siren mythology for *Siren?*

EVERSON: I had written *Covenant* and *Sacrifice*, which were demon-based novels with erotic horror overtones, and then I did another novel called *The 13th*, which was also a demon-based occult ritual book at its core. So, when I went to write a fourth book I didn't want to do yet another demon book. I wanted to branch out a bit! So, I thought . . . what kind of "monster" can I work with that hasn't been done to death and is as cool and seductive as a demon but isn't another demon book. The idea of *Siren* came from thinking about that and looking at old mythologies.

MMM: When did you first become interested in writing?

EVERSON: I've been interested in writing since I learned to write! I was a voracious reader as a kid, and early on, I realized I wanted to do for other people what my favorite authors did for me—take them to a new and strange place, and hopefully put them on the edge of their seat a few times. Give them an escape from the everyday. I thought authors were the most amazing people because they could create entire worlds, and then take me to them.

MMM: How would you classify the genre you write?

EVERSON: I write supernatural, erotic horror. Basically stories with demons, ghosts and dark magic, that tend to have sexual content. Because, well . . . you have to keep it interesting!

MMM: How do you maintain an active fascination for horror?

EVERSON: It's not really something I "try" to have, it's just something I always have loved. As a kid I watched all the classic Universal monster movies and the 50s drive-in movies that were sci-fi/horror mashups. I saw all the *Twilight Zone* and *Outer Limits* and *One Step Beyond* and *Night Gallery* episodes and then in high school discovered *Carrie* and *Firestarter* from Stephen King, which were probably my first full novel-length horror reads (I had read tons of novels prior to those, but they were mainly classic sci-fi). When I started writing short stories, sometimes they were sci-fi, but always with a nasty twist, and eventually, the sci-fi just fell away.

These days, probably the thing that keeps my interest most is discovering or rediscovering classic horror films from the '70s and 80s. I love to decompress on Friday and Saturday nights with movies, and while I can certainly point to some effective modern horror films, the stuff that really makes me horror-happy are films from that '70s-80s era, especially European horror, exploitation and giallos from Dario Argento, Lucio Fulci, Jean Rollin, Pete Walker, Umberto Lenzi, Sergio Martino, Joe D'Amato, Jess Franco, Jose Ramon Larraz and so many more.

MMM: If you could be a monster, which monster would you be and why?

EVERSON: Good question. I love Godzilla, but everyone is always shooting at him so he's always in a bad mood. I'd rather be more invisible. I guess maybe a vampire. They are often hidden, can easily seduce and get what they want, often shapeshift, and can have stupidly loyal minions. Seems like a good gig to me!

MMM: Is Castle House Asylum in *The 13th* based on any real places? Did you visit any mental hospitals when you were writing the book?

EVERSON: Honestly, it's not. And no, I've been in a lot of medical facilities, but never an asylum. The suburban Chicago town I grew up in—Tinley Park—did have a mental hospital, but it was definitely not a reconditioned old mansion in the hills of Appalachia. It did, however, lend some color to my youth—patients seemed to "escape" from there with some frequency and I remember driving to the store with my mom and seeing people walking down a busy thoroughfare in hospital gowns on occasion. The place has been shuttered for many years, but interestingly enough, just this morning I saw a news story with sad pictures of the dilapidated building talking about how the state has lost the $15 million dollars earmarked to raze the building and grounds so something else could be developed there. So, I guess there's a creepy story waiting there to be told all by itself but, it's not really what inspired *The 13th*, which is all about an old classic hotel converted to be a mental hospital.

MMM: What are your cures for Writer's Block?

EVERSON: Write? I've never really understood the term

"writer's block." I mean, I am not drowning in inspiration, but as a writer, you write. It's not about only writing when you have a brilliant idea—it's just part of your routine—you just have time set aside where you write regularly, inspired or not. When I don't have a specific idea, I'll sit down and meander a bit and then usually start down a path with a character wondering where it will lead. The discovery is what is fun about writing—I don't know any more than you do where the story is going to end up.

MMM: Which book was the easiest to write, and which book was the most difficult, and why?

EVERSON: *Covenant*, my first novel, was the hardest, because I was proving to myself that I could actually write a book. And there were several times I put it back in the drawer for a long time and said, "nope, this is too much/too hard, can't do it." So, finishing that book took me something like seven years because of all the doubt and stop-start-stops.

I'm not sure what the easiest was . . . maybe *The House by The Cemetery* because I wrote it the fastest? That one was based on a real haunted cemetery location from my childhood, so I didn't have to "make up" a lot of the mythology—there was already stuff that was real to draw from. And I had a tight deadline of about four months, so I really just dove in and knocked it out without spending too much time second guessing myself.

MMM: Tell us about your first publisher.

EVERSON: I published with a variety of magazines from 1994-2000, one of which was Delirium Magazine. When that publisher decided to launch an independent book line, they offered to issue a hardcover collection of the stories I'd been publishing throughout the '90s. The result was *Cage of Bones & Other Deadly Obsessions*, my first book. I went on to publish my first two novels with Delirium as well, *Covenant* and *Sacrifice*, along with a novelette, *Failure*. And then Leisure Books offered to reissue both of my first novels in mass market paperback, and suddenly I was reaching tens of thousands of readers rather than only a couple hundred. It was an exciting time!

MMM: I am a big fan of both Delirium Magazine and their Delirium Books. In fact, I did an interview with you in one of their magazines. Their imprint company, Corrosion Press published my first novel, *Monster Behind The Wheel*, which even made it to the Bram Stoker Final Ballot, but unfortunately didn't win. I am sorry, I digress.

EVERSON: It's okay.

MMM: Did studying journalism help you as a fiction writer?

EVERSON: I would guess so. It helped teach me the importance of clear description and not "burying the lead." Get to the point early, or you lose people. So I don't think I'm an overly "flowery" fiction writer because I don't spend a page describing the room. Hopefully, that means I move the tale along quickly.

MMM: How did winning the Stoker Award change your life?

EVERSON: It helped give my work some credibility. My name was starting to become a little familiar to genre fans at that point because I'd had dozens of stories published over the past 10 years, but the award certainly helped build on that reputation. I'm sure it helped in the decision to give my novels a shot at Leisure Books, and I know for sure the award gained me my first publishing deal in Poland—a publisher there approached me specifically because of that. They translated *Covenant* and released an initial pressing of 3,000 copies in Poland in 2007—at a time when it was only available in the United States in a 250-copy limited edition hardcover. So, at one point I had more books available in Poland than I did at home!

MMM: What do you consider your greatest accomplishment as an author?

EVERSON: It was a big thing for me to finish my first novel—*Covenant*, because I kept losing faith that I could ever finish a novel and I'd put it aside for months at a time. To have that book win the Bram Stoker Award when it was finally published was amazing. I think creatively, the greatest thing for me was writing *NightWhere*. I first thought of the idea for the novel while writing *Covenant*, but it took me a decade before I was brave enough to write the book because of the extreme themes. So, that book was a challenge to write because of what it was. And then that became a Bram Stoker Finalist and a bestseller for me in translation in Germany. So those two books are important milestones for me.

MMM: What is your opinion of the self-publishing trend?

EVERSON: It's easy, and instantly gratifying . . . but largely a dead end. Just because you can publish something on your own, doesn't mean you should. At the end of the day, if you want to reach readers, you need credibility and a marketing machine behind you to expose your work to people. Self-publishing is great if you want to say you wrote something, and it's available. But that's the easy part. Getting people to read your book when there are millions of book choices out there is the hard part. A vast amount of self-published work is poorly edited, with amateurish book covers, and has no marketing to get it exposed to readers, so it will wallow in obscurity even if the story is really good work. There are exceptions, surely. But if you want a true career as an author—convince a real publisher to put money behind your work.

MMM: Last words?

EVERSON: I have now been regularly publishing fiction for over 25 years and am starting to poke at ideas for what will be my 14th novel. I never imagined back in 1994 when my first short stories started appearing in small indie side-stapled magazines that I would ever: write a novel, see books with my name on the spine on the shelves of B&N stores, win a literary award, have my stories translated into other languages, start a small press, fly to New York to do a signing at Book Expo America, get to write a licensed *Kolchak: The Night Stalker* story, or have characters that I created appear in a Netflix series (*V-Wars*). I may never be famous or have a bestseller, but it's been a fun and unexpected second career. I'm grateful to all of the readers who have stuck with me and supported my work all this time and hope I can keep them entertained with new tales for a lot more years to come!

"Star Wars provides a vision of an alternate future that is easier for the general public to grasp than much written science-fiction. The underlying themes are not complex (deliberately so), and the films are made with respect"
—Alan Dean Foster

STAR WARS: THE FORCE AWAKENS
ALAN DEAN FOSTER

FOR OVER FIFTY YEARS Alan Dean Foster has been a professional writer. He has written in a variety of genres including science-fiction, fantasy, horror, detective, western, historical, and contemporary fiction, as well as non-fiction. He is the author of the #1 *New York Times* bestseller *Star Wars: The Force Awakens,* and the popular Flinx & Pip novels, as well as novelizations of dozens of movies, including *Star Wars*, four of the five *Alien* movies, *The Black Hole*, *Alien Nation*, *The Chronicles of Riddick*, and *Transformers*. Foster won the 2008 Grand Master award from the International Association of Media Tie-In Writers.

His novel, *Cyber Way*, won the Southwest Book Award for Fiction in 1990—the first science-fiction work ever to do so. His novel, *Shadowkeep*, was the first-ever book adaptation of an original computer game. In addition to publication in English, his books have been translated into more than fifty languages and won awards in Spain and Russia as well as the U.S.

The science-fiction writer is also an adventurer, having camped in French Polynesia and traveled to exotic spots in Europe, Asia, South America, and Africa. He has roughed it in the "Green Hell" region of the Southeastern Peruvian jungle, ridden forty-foot great white sharks in the remote waters off Western Australia, explored New Mexico's Lechuguilla Cave, and white-water-rafted the length of the Zambezi's Batoka Gorge.

Foster and his wife, JoAnn Oxley, reside in Prescott, Arizona, in a brick house that was salvaged from a turn-of-the-century miners' brothel. He is presently at work on several new novels and various media projects, including the upcoming release of *The Director Should've Shot You*, a history of his involvement with film adaptations.

You can visit his website at www.alandeanfoster.com or his fan page on Facebook.

MORE MODERN MYTHMAKERS: You have written a few *Star Wars* books in your time. You ghost-wrote the original adaptation of *Star Wars,* and you have also written *Splinter of the Mind's Eye, The Approaching Storm*, and the adaptation of *The Force Awakens*. The *Star Wars* phenomenon has been a part of popular culture now for over four decades. Why do you think everyone loves *Star Wars*?

ALAN DEAN FOSTER: A good movie is a good movie, regardless of the subject matter. Further, *Star Wars* provides a vision of an alternate future that is easier for the general public to grasp than much written science-fiction. The underlying themes are not complex (deliberately so), and the films are made with respect. The characters are equally straightforward.

MMM: For the original *Star Wars* contract, you received a $7,500 advance, and George Lucas tossed in 0.5% royalties in sales. In 2012, Walt Disney Co. bought Lucasfilm Ltd—then the royalty checks stopped. Have Disney and you reached an agreement or settlement? What can you tell us?

FOSTER: A mutually satisfactory conclusion has been reached to this issue.

MMM: Tell us how you discovered martial arts, and that aspect of your life. What was it like having Chuck Norris as a teacher?

FOSTER: When I was in the sixth grade, my parents, wanting me to be able to defend myself on the schoolyard, signed me up for a year of Judo. I enjoyed it, but not sufficiently to continue. When I finished college, I was looking for something to do besides weekend basketball to keep myself physically fit. Karate seemed interesting, so I thought I'd give it a try. At that time, Norris had a string of dojos, or schools, scattered around the Los Angeles area. He would rotate between them, occasionally giving instruction, but he also had administrative work to deal with. As I progressed upward through the basic grades, my principal instructor became Aaron Norris, Chuck's brother.

At my black belt testing, half of the judges had appeared in the seminal martial arts film *Enter the Dragon*. I was way too nervous and didn't pass. So, I'm just a 1st degree Red belt.

I attended dojos in both Santa Monica and Sherman Oaks. Steve McQueen used to come into the one in Sherman Oaks for private lessons with Chuck. I suspect he may be the one to have talked Norris into giving up his teaching business to enter show business.

MMM: How do you get out of a slump? Writing and sales-wise?

FOSTER: Writing-wise, I've never had a slump. Sales-wise? Tastes change and . . . well . . . I maintain that nothing supplants a good story, and I continue to write with that as my mantra. I will never write to the flavor of the moment or to a trend.

MMM: What is the most interesting way you killed a character in one of your books?

FOSTER: In *The Moment of the Magician*, the bad guy was slain by a kangaroo genie that emerged from the pouch of an actual (albeit sentient and talking) kangaroo.

MMM: How did you get into writing movie adaptations? Which ones do you consider your best and worst?

FOSTER: Back in the early 70s, someone at Ballantine Books had bought the book rights to a truly awful Italian film called *Luana*. Ostensibly about a female Tarzan, à la Sheena and others, in reality it featured a bunch of actors who spent most of the film walking through brush and talking silly. The female Tarzan of the title was only on screen for a small portion of the film's length and was portrayed by a dainty Vietnamese girl. A long way from Irish McCalla or even Tanya Roberts, much less the figure created by Frank Frazetta for the film's advertising campaign.

Judy-Lynn del Rey, who had taken over editorship of the science-fiction line at Ballantine, was aware that I knew my way around a film script (I have an M.F.A. in film from UCLA) and asked if I would be interested in trying to make a book out of it. Given how little there was to work with (for one thing, there was no copy of the screenplay in English), I am happy about how it turned out.

Novelizations tend to be only as good or bad as the source material. I'm particularly happy with those for *Alien* and *Dark Star* because so much of the stories take place within the minds of the characters and within single starships. I think *Transformers* also turned out well, since it gave me the opportunity to get inside the characters' heads and a bit away from the nonstop action of the film.

I'm not very happy with *Krull*, but again, you have to consider the source material. I've never turned down a novelization that I later regretted, though I'm sorry the producers of *Alien 3* forced me to change much of what I originally wrote, like exploring individual characters and their backgrounds in more depth while struggling to rationalize the obscenity of Newt's death.

MMM: You've written a number of *Star Trek* books and received a story credit for *Star Trek: The Motion Picture.* Are you a Trekker? Why do you think that Star Trek has been popular for over half a century?

FOSTER: No, I'm not a Trekker. I do like good science-fiction. As to Star Trek's popularity, it's very much a wish-fulfillment fiction in the sense that it represents a kind of general idealization of humanity, or at least the kind of humanity many people like to think we can become.

MMM: Is characterization in science fiction an empathy problem?

FOSTER: I don't think so. It's more of avoiding cliches and trying to create characters who are also different from the standard tropes. In that respect, the people I meet in my travels are an enormous help.

MMM: What are the advantages and disadvantages of writing a series?

FOSTER: They're pretty much one and the same. The

advantages include not having to create entirely new worlds or a new background, and if you wish you can utilize some or all of the same characters over and over. The disadvantages are those same things. It's very hard to keep readers interested in the same characters and the same settings book after book.

MMM: Your writing career began when August Derleth of Arkham House bought a long Lovecraftian letter of yours in 1968 and published it in the magazine, *The Arkham Collector*. How did you go from that to becoming a science-fiction novelist? And what do you think H.P. Lovecraft would make these modern times?

FOSTER: The "story" Derleth bought was actually written for fun, as a Lovecraftian pastiche-style letter. I was startled when he bought it. I thought of having the $50 check framed. That resolution lasted until my next monthly rent was due. Having finally sold a story after a dozen misfires, I subsequently sold a couple more. I then decided to try my hand at a novel, thinking that, if nothing else, it would make for good party conversation twenty years down the line ("What are you doing these days?" "Oh, I'm working on a novel . . . "). However, it [*The Tar-Aiym Krang*] sold on the third submission, to Betty Ballantine at Ballantine books, and I was off and running, or rather, typing (Smith-Corona portable electric . . . an antique today).

Lovecraft would hate the 21st Century. Too distant and too different from his preference, the 18th.

MMM: What was the inspiration for your book, *Primal Shadows*?

FOSTER: I've made three trips and spent several months in Papua New Guinea. It is in many ways the most interesting place on Earth. Certainly, the most primitive that I have had the pleasure of exploring. The people, the terrain, the wildlife is utterly fascinating, as is the history of the place. So fascinating, in fact, that when I decided to write about it, I saw no need for science-fiction embellishment, and when finally setting a story there, decided to do it as a contemporary novel and not as science-fiction. I'm very proud that people who have lived there find it an accurate and involving portrait of the country.

MMM: Several of your books featured ecological elements. Are you an environmentalist? What are some of Earth's most pressing problems, and what can be done to solve them?

FOSTER: I live on this planet. I'm stuck on it. To live here and not to be an environmentalist is to be an irresponsible passenger on a leaky boat, though there are all too many people who are quite comfortable living as slobs and fouling their own cabins. As to specific environmental problems, most can be traced to the elephant in the room that no one wants to do anything about the fact that there are simply too many people on the planet. The ship is overcrowded and under provisioned, and the next port-of-call is a long way over the spatial horizon.

Short of solving that overlying conundrum, the most immediate problem we need to deal with is rapid climate change. I hold out great hope for the ongoing transition to electrically-driven modes of transportation and power. We need to continue to expand our solar and wind generating capacity. It's absurd that Denmark can do it and the U.S. cannot. Pollution: too many non-biodegradable containers, insufficient conservation of water (if 80 percent plus goes to agriculture, that means saving 20 percent would allow for a doubling of supply to every other consuming source), and chemical pollution.

MMM: Some of your villains' downfalls are a lack of respect for alien species. What is it about this theme that appeals to you?

FOSTER: There is a regrettable tendency for us as individuals, as well as a species, to consider ourselves innately superior to others. Having traveled extensively, I know that it's usually the small things that get you; the dangers that are overlooked. You're far less likely to die being eaten by a shark or a lion than you are from contracting a disease or internal parasite. There are all kinds of superiority. H.G. Wells recognized this when he had his invading Martians defeated by common germs. The U.S. may subside as an international power not due to defeat in war, but by having our economic vitality sapped through a combination of stupid policies, a rejection of logic and science, and outright corruption.

MMM: As a world traveler, you have visited some exotic locales. What are some of your favorites?

FOSTER: Favorites? I've already mentioned New Guinea. Anywhere in the Pacific. Prague, St. Petersburg, Rome, London, Vienna, Heidelberg... I could list cities endlessly. I adore Turkey and India. Africa is always surprising. Australia is like being home, but with different swear words. New Zealand is the most beautiful country I've ever visited. The Arctic is rejuvenating. South America is an unending cornucopia of wonders and charming people.

MMM: You've written over a hundred books and hundreds of short stories. How do you keep your writing fresh? How do you maintain an active fascination for the genres? Is there a fear you'll run out of ideas eventually?

FOSTER: To a professional writer, everything and anything is a subject for a story. As to keeping fresh, after decades it becomes difficult. I try to challenge myself from time to time by tackling a genre in which I rarely work, such as historical fiction, or even songwriting. As to the genres, well, it's impossible to be bored by science-fiction, or to run out of ideas. The problem is too many ideas, not a lack of them.

MMM:Last words?

FOSTER: Isn't that premature? Oh, you mean for the purposes of this interview. I simply enjoy telling stories. I have no illusions about being read in the far future. There was a time when I worried about critical recognition and such things. Now I am only concerned with what the readers think. For the past year I've been writing orchestral music. I think that for any creative person a little occasionally reinvention is exhilarating.

As to actual Last Words, well, here's how I want my epitaph to read:

"Earth."
"Been there. Done That."

"While the horror genre is not my only interest, I consider it home. I read and watch all kinds of stuff, but horror is where my heart is. The genre is much maligned, but it never goes out of style."

—Ray Garton

SEX AND VIOLENCE IN HOLLYWOOD
RAY GARTON

BY PAMELA BRIGGS, DAVID KEMPF & MICHAEL MCCARTY

RAY GARTON IS the popular, award-winning author of over sixty books. He has been praised by Peter Straub, Stephen King, Harlan Ellison, Ramsey Campbell, Joe Lansdale, and Dean Koontz.

A fairly normal California childhood didn't stop Ray Garton from writing dark, sexually charged, wickedly violent novels with vampires, ghosts, werewolves, and everything in between.

In addition to movie tie-ins that include the *Nightmare on Elm Street* series *and Buffy the Vampire Slayer*, he has written numerous original horror novels. In 2006, Ray was presented with the World Horror Convention Grand Master Award. He lives in Northern California with his wife Dawn, and his cats.

MORE MODERN MYTHMAKERS: Why is horror a good genre for you? You have written horror, science fiction, noir, but why do you keep returning back to horror?

RAY GARTON: Horror works for me because I was a Seventh-day Adventist, a very bizarre religion that was, quite frankly, horrific in its teachings and beliefs. I was traumatized by that religion at a very young age. My attraction to the horror genre was a natural outgrowth of that because my life was filled with horror, thanks to the church. Fiction in general, and horror specifically are forbidden to Adventists, but ironically, it was Adventism that made me a horror writer.

MMM: You have said in the past that your religious upbringing was full of obsession over the end of the world and fear. How much of an impact did the church have on you?

GARTON: My upbringing had a lot to do with my interest in horror, although I didn't realize it at the time. I saw my first horror movie on TV when I was about five years old. It was *13 Ghosts*. By that time, I was already living in fear of the "time of trouble" that's such an important part of Seventh-day Adventist doctrine. I regularly had nightmares that would disrupt my sleep, and I would sometimes lie awake at night in bed, either praying that god would kill me before that time came, or trying to decide how best to kill myself once it arrived. That movie scared the hell out of me, but it was a fun kind of scary. I enjoyed it. It channeled the fear that was bottled up inside me.

After that, I sought out more horror on TV, and I discovered horror comic books, and later, novels and short stories. But this only caused more trouble for me because Sadventism (as I call it) prohibits the reading of fiction. I understand that these days, they have a much harder time dictating that particular rule, but the cult's prophet and founder, Ellen G. White, wrote that god showed her that reading fiction could actually cause health problems, physical paralysis, and mental illness. So I got a lot of flak for my interests. In fact, I was reminded almost daily that my interests were a sign that there was something wrong with me; that Satan was working hard on me. I always had a need to tell stories. I don't know why. Before I could write, I drew them in comic strip panels. Then I learned to write and I was always writing stories, one after another, and they all tended to be dark. Most fell in the horror genre. This, I was told, was a sign that Satan was working through me. Being told that sort of thing all the time, day after day, resulted in a lot of self-loathing.

MMM: Did it impact your work politically and philosophically as well as personally?

GARTON: No, I don't think so.

MMM: You also said that you believe you got a pretty good break into the writing business, do you think it's more difficult to make fiction writing your sole source of income these days?

GARTON: I was very lucky in that horror fiction was extremely popular when I was starting out. I sold my first novel when I was 20. It was published in 1984, in the middle of the horror fiction boom. If I were starting out today — well, the very thought makes me shudder. Things are a lot different now. Not only has horror never recovered from the collapse of its mainstream popularity in the early '90s, but publishing itself bears little resemblance to the business when I started out. I don't envy anyone who's starting out right now. There are a lot of new avenues that writers can take, but writers have to do all their own marketing, and good luck getting attention. These days, everybody and their plumber has a book to sell. It seems if you're not hawking a book, you're some kind of slacker. Everybody's doing it.

MM. In *The New Neighbor* you wrote about a strange neighbor. Have you lived near any real strange neighbors before, or are you the strange neighbor?

GARTON: We've been extraordinarily lucky. We've either gotten along well with our neighbors or they've quietly kept to themselves. Right now, we have the best neighbors we've ever had in our 33 years together. We've all gotten to know each other and become friends, and we watch each other's houses when someone goes on a trip.

The New Neighbor was set in the first neighborhood Dawn and I lived in together where there was a woman who seemed to think the other women in the neighborhood were out to seduce her husband away from her. There was no truth to that suspicion because her husband certainly was no catch. But it made me wonder what it would be like if a beautiful woman moved in who *did* sexually prey on all the husbands on the street. And that developed into *The New Neighbor*.

MMM: What was the inspiration for *The Loveliest Dead*?

GARTON: *The Loveliest Dead* was inspired by experience writing the so-called "non-fiction" book *In A Dark Place: The Story Of A True Haunting*, with ghost-hunting demonologist frauds Ed and Lorraine Warren. The ghost-hunting ghoul in the novel was heavily inspired by the Warrens.

MMM: Do you enjoy mentoring or helping new writers in the horror genre?

GARTON: I'm always willing to answer questions and offer encouragement and, if I have any advice to new writers, whether they work in the genre or not. I got a lot of kind encouragement and advice from writers when I was starting out, and I'm always eager to do the same for others. I don't have the time to read manuscripts, and legally, that's a bad idea for any professional writer. But, I always try to make myself available to up-and-coming writers.

MMM: Tell us about your daily (or nightly) working routine.

GARTON: My routine seems to morph with each project. Right now, I'm writing in the late afternoon and evening. I usually take a break to spend some time with my wife in the evening. And then I get back to work when she goes to bed. While I'm writing, I usually have music playing, or a movie running on the TV. It has to be a movie I've seen many times, though, something I'm familiar with so it doesn't become a distraction. I like the noise, though.

MM. What is the hardest part of being a professional writer?

GARTON: My answers to this question and the next one are going to be related. For me, the hardest part of being a professional writer has been trying to protect my work and my ability to do it from the constant distractions and intrusions of real life. Family upheavals, health problems, money problems, having to move, a cluster of personal disasters of various stripes—things like that are constantly clawing and biting at your attention, demanding time spent away from work, shattering concentration, deflating enthusiasm for the work, and generally sucking at the energy that needs to be expended on work. Everyone has them, and some deal with them better than others, but finding the balance needed to successfully juggle writing and real life is an important and often frustrating demand made of every writer.

MMM: How do you get out of a slump? Writing and sales-wise?

GARTON: One way of *avoiding* a writing slump is to write Every. Single. Day. Without. Exception. Never let a day pass without writing *something*. Because that keeps you in the habit of putting your butt in the seat and working, which is the *only* way to be a writer. There are no shortcuts around that. Developing, and then clinging to that habit is one of the most important parts of writing—maybe *the* most important—and it's rarely discussed. I know the importance of this habit from cold, bitter experience.

I'm in a slump right now. Bad health has made writing extremely difficult. For one thing, I can't sit for very long without having intense pain. This has shattered my ability to focus on what I'm writing. Thanks to these health problems, I fell out of that all-important habit of writing something every day. For the last few years, I've been trying to get back into that habit. *For the last few years*! And I still haven't mastered it. That's still due in part to my health problems, but part of the problem is that I lost sight of that daily habit. And getting back into it is hard as hell, I can tell you.

As for sales slumps—I've found that I can either pay attention to sales and the business end, or I can write, but I've found it very hard to do both. Some have a real talent for it, but for me it's been a struggle. The whole experience of trying to focus on that end of things has felt like a slump.

MMM: Of all the books you've written so far. What three books are your favorite?

GARTON: *Live Girls* because it was, and still is, my most successful and famous novel (a movie is currently in the works—again), and some may say my best. *Scissors* because it contains more of *me* than any other horror novel I've written. My absolute favorite of all my novels is *Sex and Violence in Hollywood* (being adapted for the screen by Charlie Matthau), which is not horror, but a sort of black comedy/thriller—because it showed me exactly what I can accomplish in a book when I really put my mind to it. I seem to be leaning more toward the flavor of *Sex and Violence in Hollywood* in my work than horror these days.

MMM: For *Live Girls* you traveled to New York City and for *Crucifax* you went to the San Fernando Valley. What other places did you go to research your novels?

GARTON: The truth is, I travel very little for research. I started with *Live Girls* during my first visit to New York, after a trip to a peep show in then-sleazy Times Square. When I wrote *Crucifax*, I was living in the San Fernando Valley. I tend to set most of my fiction in places where I've spent time—San Francisco, Los Angeles, the Napa Valley, and my now town of Anderson, California. Or, I just make the place up, as I've done with Big Rock, California, in *Ravenous*.

MMM: Is "Everything Must Go" (in the Cemetery Dance anthology *Midnight Premiere*) a tribute to backwoods horror movies such as *The Hills Have Eyes* and *Texas Chainsaw Massacre*?

GARTON: Yes, it's a direct nod to those movies and the many knock-offs and remakes they inspired. That is a very specific sub-genre in horror, and I think those two movies have had more to do with creating it than anything else.

MMM: What is a Lot Lizard? And why did you decide to write about this subject in *Lot Lizards*?

GARTON: A lot lizard is truck stop hooker—they hang around the back lot where the trucks are parked and hit on the truckers, either for money or drugs. They're pretty skanky too. I used to write late into the night at a truck stop restaurant, and when I first learned of lot lizards, I knew there was a book title in that somewhere.

MMM: Let's talk about a couple of your other books. I'm a big fan of *'Nids* and *Biofire*. What would you like to say about these novels?

GARTON: *'Nids* was a nostalgic book for me, an affectionate nod to the countless monster movies I spent so much of my childhood watching on TV. I still have so much love for those creaky old movies, something that will be understood perfectly by anyone who grew up a misfit and found a second home among the monsters. It's not that I was such a weirdo back then, but I grew up in a very cloistered, strict, fundamentalist Christian environment in which I did not fit or belong and, as a result, I spent a lot of time alone, and monsters were my friends. Every now and then, I'll write something that acknowledges my gratitude to those monsters. *'Nids* was the first one, I think. *Crawlers* was another.

I've always been fascinated with the idea of someone being able to kill with a single thought. No special effects or pyrotechnics, just a thought, followed by an opened aorta or a quiet embolism. By the time I wrote *Biofire*, the idea had been bouncing around in my head for a long time, and I finally sat down and decided to do something with it. I took that opportunity to do something else I'd been wanting to try: set a story in a big, dark, unnamed, fictional city. That's where *Biofire* is set. I originally conceived the story as a thriller involving numerous sinister representatives of various governments around the world killing each other to get to this new weapon. But ultimately, I ended up with a smaller, tighter book that was set, in part, in the lab where Biofire is developed, a lab full of some really messed up people. While the psychic weapon is the main focus, the protagonist is surrounded by a host of selfish, menacing characters with their own personal agendas.

MMM: How do you maintain an active fascination for horror after all these years?

GARTON: That has taken no effort at all. While the horror genre is not my only interest, I consider it home. I read and watch all kinds of stuff, but horror is where my heart is. The genre is much maligned, but it never goes out of style, not really. Its popularity waxes and wanes, but it never goes away. Everybody enjoys a good scare. And I think people get more out of a good horror novel or movie than they're aware of getting. It's a release, a chance to safely face death and walk away from it unharmed.

And horror can be just as socially conscious as any other genre. It can comment on the times in which we live as effectively as science fiction. Or it can be pure escapism, something that never gets the credit it deserves. I think escapism is an actual necessity, especially in the weird and worrying times in which we find ourselves now. That's something that I think all good art provides. It picks us up and takes us away from ourselves, our surroundings, our lives, and relocates us somewhere else for a while, someplace where we can forget, for a time, the troubles we left back home.

MMM: How do you come up with the original plots and characters you create?

GARTON: First of all, I try to avoid doing what's already been done. For example, I wouldn't go near zombies right now. Everybody's doing zombies. I'm not crazy about that subgenre, anyway, but right now, I want to hurl every time I see a new zombie novel or collection or movie. Enough, already! The plots are usually determined, to a certain extent, by the characters. And the characters are drawn from my own personal experiences with people. I don't mean that they're based on specific people, because they aren't. They come from my experience with people in general.

MMM: If you could be a monster. What monster would you be and why?

GARTON: Well, whether or not I'm *already* a monster depends entirely on who you talk to. Ha! That's a question I've never been asked in an interview before and I've been giving it a lot of thought before answering. It's a hard one to answer because, to be honest, I wouldn't *want* to be a monster. There seems to be two kinds of monsters in horror. If I were the kind that had no humanity in it whatsoever, if I were just a pure, unredeemable monster, I would end up hurting and killing a lot of people, and depending on which monster I was, I might even end up *eating* them. Exactly *none* of that appeals to me.

On the other hand, if I were the kind of monster who retained some humanity and didn't really *want* to hurt anyone, a hapless monster who finds himself in a world and a situation he did not create and doesn't fully understand— a monster like Frankenstein's creature or Larry Talbot in *The Wolf Man*—I would be *miserable*. That makes it a difficult question to answer. I think we all have both of those monsters inside of us in one form or another. Under the right circumstances, which would by necessity be extremely unpleasant, I think most of us could become that unredeemable monster that just wants to break things and hurt people. Pushed to the right extremes, under the right grueling circumstances, I think that monster might come out of us. And at one time or another, I think we've all felt like that ugly, misunderstood beast who doesn't really *want* to hurt anyone, who doesn't fit anywhere or who is rejected in a big way. I think that's what makes monsters so appealing—they're really a part of us.

And I'm afraid that is an evasive, noncommittal answer is the best I can do with this question.

MMM: Why do you think horror films and books remain relatively popular?

GARTON: Their popularity never dies, although it does experience surges from time to time. Watching a horror movie or reading horror fiction are two of the only ways we can put ourselves in safe danger, confront and survive death, be terrified without risking our injury or death, and walk away with a great feeling of relief. They're our way of having nightmares when we're awake. When they're done right, they fill that need.

MMM: You advised young writers ``writing is not something you go to school to learn, it is something you dropout of school and do." Can you elaborate?

GARTON: That was probably an irresponsible thing to say— I said it a long time ago. It refers to my own personal experience. I dropped out of college to write. Now, though, I often wish I'd stuck it out and had something to fall back on in the dry periods.

MMM: What non-horror writers do you like reading?

GARTON: I'm a huge fan of John Jakes, the poignant novels

of Anne Tyler, and everything John Irving writes. People are surprised when they learn this about me.

MMM: Is it true you like to write with a rough outline—not too detailed, just to keep subplots from stealing focus. Do you have the luxury of writing and just let yourself write, see what happens and maybe save the extra ideas for another project? Or do deadlines prohibit such indulgences?

GARTON: Actually, the main reason I do very little outlining is that once I've finished a complete and detailed outline of a book. I don't want to write the book, because it feels like I already have—I feel like I'm already done with it. What I typically do is start with an idea, write for a while, then stop and outline a few chapters ahead, go back and write the chapters, then start the process all over again until I'm done. This keeps me focused without giving me the feeling that I've already written the book before it's written.

MMM: Last words?

GARTON: Hardly a day goes by that I don't realize how fortunate I am to be doing for a living the only thing I've ever wanted to do with my life. That has been *entirely* due to the people who faithfully continue to read and spread the word about my work. I will be *deeply* indebted to them for the rest of my life, and I just wanted to take this opportunity to say so.

"Everyone gets scared or has a phobia or a line they won't cross, everyone gets attracted to things they shouldn't, even if they don't act on them, everyone experiences temptation . . . I feel that erotica and horror are familiar places for everyone, whether you admit or not"

—Sèphera Girón

MISTRESS OF THE DARK
SÈPHERA GIRÓN

SÈPHERA GIRÓN WAS born in New Orleans and currently makes her home in Toronto. She has published four books with Leisure, three with Samhain Horror, plus there's her *Witch Upon a Star* series with Riverdale Avenue Books among others. You can find her books and stories online, in bookstores, and even on phone apps!

Sèphera also enjoys exploring haunted houses and has stayed overnight at the Lizzie Borden Bed and Breakfast in Massachusetts numerous times with other horror writers. She was also part of a group of horror writers who attended the Haunted Mansion Retreat in California twice, which spawned two anthologies, and she has been to the Stanley Hotel Writers Retreat in Colorado.

When Sèphera isn't writing, she's teaching budding writers at a local college.

MORE MODERN MYTHMAKERS: I know you've probably

heard this a million times before, but Sèphera is a pretty name. What does your name mean? Why did your parents choose that name? And do you think that's a good name for a horror writer?

SÈPHERA GIRÓN: When my parents were pregnant with me, they saw the movie *The Ten Commandments*. They loved the name, which in that movie is Moses' wife. In those days, there was no Google, so they created their own spelling. I find it amusing as Yvonne De Carlo played "Sephera" in the movie and then went on to be Lily Munster. I added the accent so people would say it correctly.

In my thirties, in studying the metaphysical and occult arts with a teacher, I learned about the Tree of Life/Kabbalah and sephiroth/sefirot and that all blew my mind. My parents didn't consciously name me after all of that, but they agree it's all quite interesting.

MMM: *The Birds and The Bees* is a nature run amok novel. Why did you decide to write in that sub-genre?

GIRÓN: At the time that I wrote that, I had a fear of birds, and killer bees were on the way, and I thought it would be fun to write a huge apocalyptic book. While I was writing the book, 9/11 happened and I went into a deep depression, as did most of North America, I'm sure. The book changed directions from my original intent, but it still was fun to write!

MMM: Women writing dark erotica are judged harder than men writing in the same field. Agree or disagree and why?

GIRÓN: I've never really thought about it too deeply about myself. I think that's why I keep on writing. I see stories on Twitter and Facebook all the time about this writer or that writer "quitting horror" because "the genre isn't supportive" or people "tweeted at them!" and now they must quit their supposed passion. If you have a passion, no one can take it away from you, it comes from within.

Writing horror is no different than writing any other genre nor is being a writer any harder than any other job. You do your job or don't. You listen to the naysayers who want to drag you down or you don't. You don't have to read your tweets or email if people are being nasty to you. And why do you care what "they" think? "They" are obviously not your readers.

I've been working in horror professionally for over twenty years. It's never been "easy" for women no matter what you're writing. In fact, these days it's super easy for women as everyone wants to include women in their anthologies and line-ups so that they look diverse. This is the easiest time in history for women to write and publish horror, dark fantasy, science fiction, erotica, and so on.

But back to the original thought . . . as a woman writing dark erotica, horror, science fiction . . . you either grow a thick skin and suck it up, or you cry and quit. I love writing too much to let some bullies force me to quit. People will judge you no matter what you do and that's life!

MMM: House of Pain is a very creepy haunted house book. What was the inspiration for that novel?

GIRÓN: *House of Pain* was originally written as a screenplay for an indie film director/producer looking for horror scripts. The screenplay was too big for his budget, so he passed. However, I ultimately pitched the idea to Leisure Books, and it became my first book with Leisure.

I have to say, as a writer, adapting a screenplay to a book was the best fun I've ever had. The skeleton of the book was there, I just had to bring it to life!

The springboard of the idea was taken from the Paul Bernardo/Karla Homolka case that was going on at the time. They had been caught, the trials were going on, and the torture house was bulldozed. In Canada, we had news blackouts about the trial so we couldn't know anything until it was all over. Obviously before social media times!

My book opens with the bulldozing of the torture house although *House of Pain* features fictional serial killers loosely based on Bernardo and Homolka. At the time, it was considered too horrifying to actually write about them. Also, the book isn't about them, it's about a different character, they are just the evil backdrop.

Also, at the time, Leisure editor Don D'Auria wanted me to change the setting of my book from Ontario, where the case actually happened, to the States as back in those days, readers only wanted their horror based in the US. The industry has changed tons since those days. I've worked with Don on several books since at a couple of houses, and now have published books set in Toronto.

I also was doing a lot of metaphysical studies at the time and so there is a lot of that in there. I also love monsters, like Audrey 2 in *Little Shop of Horrors*, so THAT was an inspiration as well.

MMM: Why do you think dark erotica and horror work so well together?

GIRÓN: Everyone gets scared or has a phobia or a line they won't cross, everyone gets attracted to things they shouldn't even if they don't act on them, everyone experiences temptation . . . I feel that erotica and horror are familiar places for everyone, whether you admit it or not.

In a story, you can cross lines and see where the choice might take you to which you can't or shouldn't do in real life.

MMM: How do you maintain an active fascination for horror?

GIRÓN: I've always had a dark side, a fascination with "what if?" and "why?" My first poems as a child were about squirrels getting hit by cars and lying twitching and bleeding by the side of the road. I still love squirrels. I collect Scrats if anyone has any extras, they want to send me!

I like to peek into the shadows and see what's there. The type of horror I enjoy consuming changes as I change. A story like *The Shining* still haunts me to this day, partly because that horror had many levels. The ghosts, the hedge animals, the dark side of human nature, an intangible entity, temptation, magic . . .

I'm not as interested these days in slice and dice, and I've not seen any of *The Purge* movies as I think they would be too scary for me. Yet, I love the *Human Centipede* movies.

I like to see what people will come up with next.

MMM: If you could be a monster, which monster would you be and why?

GIRÓN: That's a tough one. If I had to be an evil humanoid-type monster, I'd pick the Kylo Ren from *Star Wars 9: The Force Awakens*, the evil with potential and more power than he knows. Not the Kylo Ren from the movies that followed where he becomes a lovesick puppy dog wimp.

I might be Loki from the new Marvel movies, another human-type monster. I've been binge-watching the *Loki* series and just watched all the *Thor* movies this week. He'd be a cool tormented horrible person to become in order to spread evil and mischief around the world and galaxy.

If I was a non-human monster, I'd like to be a Megalodon that could fly . . . a sharknado?

MMM: What is the best advice another writer has ever given you?

GIRÓN: "Just keep writing" is the general blanket one.

In asking best-selling novelist Heather Graham (on one of our visits to the Lizzie Borden Bed and Breakfast) how she keeps writing so many books, her response was, "I don't know how to do anything else to earn a living, so I have to keep writing!" that also resonates with me.

MMM: Of all the books you've written, which one was the easiest to write and which one the most difficult to write?

GIRÓN: I guess my first book that got published, not the first book that I wrote, would have been the hardest. I spent almost ten years writing and rewriting it, not knowing if I'd ever be published ever. That was *Eternal Sunset.*

The *Witch Upon a Star* books are the easiest to write as I have outlines and character sheets for all the characters in the series.

MMM: Why do Tarot card readings play a recurring theme in your work?

GIRÓN: I began my relationship with the tarot in my thirties and find it an endlessly fascinating tool both in my writing and in my real life. I always have a deck on my desk.

MMM: Vanessa has appeared in your books *Borrowed Flesh* and *Eternal Sunset?* Is she in any of your other books and will she be so in the future?

GIRÓN: When I first wrote about Vanessa, I saw her as a character that could last across a series of books (movies, and TV shows!), if anyone ever wanted to read them. When *Eternal Sunset* was published by DarkTales Books, they were going to publish the trilogy, which included *Eternal Nightmare* and *Eternal Dreamers.* However, DarkTales went under and to this day, no one seems interested in *Eternal Sunset* and the next books. I was able to write about Vanessa as a much older witch in *Borrowed Flesh (Leisure),* so it was fun to work with her again.

In these modern times, my original ideas for the *Eternal* books likely won't work anymore, so it's time to move on. Vanessa may or may not make appearances in future books.

Like many writers with a body of work, all my books are connected, some in obvious ways, some not so much. So, there's always a possibility that Vanessa and some of the others will return one day.

MMM: Last words?

GIRÓN: During the pandemic, I returned to my screenwriting roots. I studied screenwriting and filmmaking in university and had a couple of small successes way back in the day. So, during the pandemic, I took countless screenwriting webinars, bought Final Draft and I've been working on two TV show pilots and a couple of screenplays, not all horror, and have entered a few contests. I had started my writing path as a screenwriter, but then when I was able to sell books, I focused more on that. Now I'm dabbling in both worlds. It's a big dream to have one of my TV shows or movies come to life, so I hope that maybe a director or producer will find my work interesting enough to take a chance on me! I wouldn't object to any of my books or stories being adapted either!

I'm a big believer in following modern technology, so my three books that were originally published by Samhain Horror and edited by Don D'Auria are now on the SCREAM app. As of this writing, I'm working on an original fun witchy book that I hope will go on the app as well.

I'm working on another horror novel that is very dark that I hope to pitch to a traditional publisher. I have submitted pitches to another online app where if I'm accepted, my horror book will be like a choose your adventure-type game. I'm curious about that format as well.

Last words to writers are:

Write, write, write. Don't listen to the negative people who want to bring you down. If you don't believe in yourself and your work, no one else will either.

Also, ladies, be proud of your real names and use them. Please stop hiding behind initials and man-names, we'll never be accepted as serious horror writers unless we stand proud, beginning with our names.

http://sepheragiron.ca
http://www.youtube.com/sephera
http://www.twitter.com/sephera
http://www.instagram.com/sepheragiron
http://www.twitch.tv/sephera666

"I have written a lot of things other than horror, but it is the scary stuff I enjoy writing the most. Having a reader say I scared the hell out of them never gets old."
—Owl Goingback

TRIBAL SCREAMS
OWL GOINGBACK

OWL GOINGBACK HAS been writing professionally for over thirty years, and is the author of numerous novels, children's books, screenplays, magazine articles, short stories, and comics. He is an HWA Lifetime Achievement Award Recipient, a two-time Bram Stoker Award Winner (for novel and first novel), and a Nebula Award Nominee. His books include *Crota, Darker Than Night, Evil Whispers, Breed, Shaman Moon, Coyote Rage, Tribal Screams, Eagle Feathers,* and *The Gift.*

In addition to writing under his own name, Owl has ghostwritten books for Hollywood celebrities. He has also lectured across the country on the customs and folklore of the American Indians, served in the military, owned a restaurant/lounge, and worked as a cemetery caretaker.

MORE MODERN MYTHMAKERS: The Bram Stoker Award is one of the highest honors a horror writer can get. How did it feel to win the First Novelist Award for *Crota*?

OWL GOINGBACK: Absolutely amazing. It is hard to put into words how elated I was about winning, because the book had come so close to never making it into print. *Crota* had been rejected by a dozen publishers before being accepted. And when my agent finally sold it, the novel almost didn't get released. At the time, the publishing house that bought it, Donald I. Fine Books, was being acquired by Penguin/Putnam, Mr. Fine was also dying of cancer, and the editor assigned to *Crota* quit to become a real estate agent. Everything that could go wrong did, so it is a miracle the book made it into stores.

Luckily, *Crota* did get published and the reviews were good. I guess a lot of my peers also liked the story because it wound up being the first book ever nominated for a Bram Stoker Award in two different categories: first novel and novel. Of course, I was up against Stephen King's *The Green Mile* in the novel category, so there was no way in hell I was going to win both awards.

The awards ceremony that year was held in New York City, and I was in a room with some of the biggest names in the horror genre. Heck, sitting at our table was Ira Levin, author of *Rosemary's Baby*. I was so starstruck, I don't think I spoke more than two words to him.

Luck was with me that night in more ways than one because also sitting at our table was an editor with Signet Books. *Crota* had only been published in hardback, so I started talking to him about a follow-up paperback deal. As a matter of fact, when I won the award for First Novel, I set the trophy in front of him. The trick worked; not only did Signet bring out the paperback edition of *Crota*, but they also bought my next three novels as paperback originals.

MMM: Is the Skinwalker Legend an inspiration for *Coyote Rage* or were you inspired by something else?

GOINGBACK: It is one of the inspirations, but certainly not the only one. I was familiar with the Navajo stories about Skinwalkers, and their beliefs that witches could turn their skins inside out or wear the skins of others. The belief in Skinwalkers and shapeshifters still exists today. I have never seen one myself but know others who swear they have had encounters. All I know is that there are things out there that cannot be explained.

But I was also inspired by the Trickster stories of different indigenous tribes, with Coyote, Raven, and Rabbit taking the title role in those stories. The Trickster is a villain but can also be a hero; it all depends on the story. He is mischievous, a known troublemaker, but always interesting. In *Coyote Rage*, I wanted to make Coyote a shapeshifter, and I wanted to make him cunning and dangerous. He is out to destroy mankind's reign in this world.

MMM: Is the Tolomato Cemetery in your book *Breed* modeled after any real abandoned graveyards?

GOINGBACK: Tolomato Cemetery is a real place. It is an old catholic cemetery in historic St. Augustine, Florida. The cemetery was built on the former site of a Guale Indian village and is believed by many to be haunted. As a matter of fact, what I captured on film one night at the Tolomato is the reason I wrote *Breed*.

I love the historic area of St. Augustine, especially at night. Usually after 10:00 pm the streets are empty, and you have the place pretty much to yourself. One night I was taking photos around midnight at the Tolomato. A neighboring business had left their gate open, so I was able to get around on the backside of the cemetery. Sticking my 35 mm camera up to the fence, I snapped several quick shots. When I developed the film, I noticed in one of the photos there was a green beam of light in an area where no electrical lights had existed. The beam was striking one of the above ground crypts and standing in it was a woman. I could see her, but I could also see through her. She was wearing an 1800s style wedding dress, complete with a half veil. She faced the grave, but her eyes were staring into my camera. She did not look happy.

Seeing the photo piqued my interest into the history and hauntings of old St. Augustine. I started interviewing the locals, and it turns out dozens of people claim to have seen the woman I captured on film. They call her the bride because, according to the legend, she died a week before her wedding and was buried in her bridal gown.

St. Augustine is the only place I have ever been where all the locals seem to have a ghost story, even the former mayor and chief of police. I caught a lot of strange things on film during my research, and had some really creepy experiences, so I just had to write a novel about the place.

MMM: Was *Crota* your tribute to Grade-B monster movies? If so, what are some of your favorite "Creature Features?"

GOINGBACK: Yes, it was. I was a huge monster kid growing up; still am. I read every copy of *Famous Monsters of Filmland* I could get my hands on, built all of the monster model kits, and stayed up until the wee hours of the night to watch old Creature Feature films. I love all the classic Universal horror films, along with the giant bug movies of the 1950s. *Crota* was written in homage to those monster movies.

Creature from the Black Lagoon has to be my all-time favorite monster film. Not only was the Creature itself so unique, and visibly stunning, but they put so much work into the backstory to make the film believable. Ricou Browning, who played the Creature in all the underwater scenes, did an amazing job making the Gill-man look real.

MMM: If you could be any monster, what would it be and why?

GOINGBACK: When I was young, I always thought it would be fun to be a werewolf. For a few days each month, I could put aside my normal life and literally run wild. I could be a lone wolf, or part of a pack. Best of all, I could take care of all the bullies and troublemakers who made my adolescence miserable.

But I just wrote a Dracula story for the anthology *Classic Monsters Unleashed*, so now I am thinking that being a vampire might be a better choice. Vampires get to live in cool gothic castles, with libraries full of ancient books; they attend great masquerade balls, and never have to go out in the heat of day—a good thing here in the balmy state of Florida. Best of all, they can turn into a wolf anytime they want. No waiting for the full moon to don fur and fangs.

MMM: Of all the horror books you've written so far. Which one was the easiest to write? And which one was the hardest? And why?

GOINGBACK: I think *Evil Whispers* was probably the easiest to write, because all of the action takes place in one location. It is set at a fish camp here in central Florida, so I didn't have to do extensive research for background details. I also did not have to spend days studying police procedures, crime scene investigations, or how to properly prepare a body for burial as I did in *Crota*, *Breed*, and *Coyote Rage*.

Breed was probably the hardest to write because there were so many little background details I had to get right. Being set in the historic St. Augustine, Florida, I needed to get all of the locations and street names right. I also needed to be knowledgeable about the city's history, no easy task when you are talking about a place that has experienced everything from deadly hurricanes to pirate invasions. And that was just for background details. Since one of the main characters was a ghost tour guide, I had to study up on St. Augustine's hauntings and ghostly legends. I also needed to take a refresher course in crime scene investigations, because technology had greatly improved since writing *Crota*.

MMM: How do you get out of a slump? With writing and sales?

GOINGBACK: Normally, I would say getting out of a writing slump is just a matter of putting words on paper. But then the pandemic hit and a lot of writers, myself included, found themselves in a Covid slump. It is hard to concentrate on writing tales of terror when the whole world is experiencing a real-life horror story. But now there is a vaccine, and hope is on the horizon, so my slump is a thing of the past and I am back to a normal writing schedule.

Now that we are getting the pandemic under control, I would again say getting out of a slump can best be accomplished by not giving up. Force your mind to work through the problem. If the words still refuse to come then take a walk, get some fresh air, and have a go at it again. Do not overthink things, just let the writing flow. Good stories tell themselves; we are just the vessels lucky enough to receive them.

MMM: How important is it for a new writer to get an agent these days?

GOINGBACK: I honestly do not think a writer needs an agent when first starting out. I didn't seek out an agent until after I had contracts in hand for two children's books with a major publishing company. Then I sought an agent, because the contracts were so complicated, I needed someone to protect my interest. If I had not gotten an agent at that time, then I would have hired a lawyer to go over the contracts.

MMM: How do you maintain an active fascination for horror?

GOINGBACK: I love horror. A good horror novel or book is like the thrill of a roller coaster without the dizziness and annoying vomiting. It is the only genre where I have just as much fun reading a book, or watching a movie, for a second or third time.

I have written a lot of things other than horror, but it is the scary stuff I enjoy writing the most. Having a reader say I scared the hell out of them never gets old.

MMM: What advice would you give a new writer in horror?

GOINGBACK: If you want to be a good writer, then take time to perfect your craft. Study plot techniques, character development, and viewpoints. Read the masters to find out what makes them great. And do the necessary research to make the unbelievable seem real. Finally, write, write, write; you will only get better through practice.

MMM: Last words?

GOINGBACK: Being a writer is not easy. It takes determination and a lot of hard work. It is definitely not a career for the faint of heart, or for those with thin skins. But if you are dedicated, and willing to put in the hours to hone your craft, then the rewards can be amazing. There is nothing in this world that compares to seeing your name as a byline in a magazine, at the beginning of a movie, or on the cover of a book. The only thing better is knowing you scared the hell out of someone.

"The copy editor said, 'Mulder wouldn't say that.' I wrote a note back and said, 'Look at the show, he's swearing all the time.' According to Chris Carter I didn't get Mulder and Scully right. Carter said the two books (Goblins *and* Whirlwind) *were 'noir; which is dark and he said* The X-Files *wasn't"*
—Charles Grant

THE SOFT WHISPER OF THE DEAD
CHARLES L. GRANT

BY CRISTOPHER DEROSE & MICHAEL MCCARTY

CHARLES L. GRANT HAS BEEN writing classic quiet horror for 35 years. Charles is well known to speculative fiction fans, readers, and writers alike and has considerable respect since the release of his 1976 debut, *The Shadow Of Alpha*. He has also written such novels and short story collections as *In A Dark Dream, The Long Night Of The Grave, The Soft Whisper Of The Dead, The Dark Cry Of The Moon, For Fear Of The Night, Dialing The Wind, Night Seasons, Night Songs,* and many more.

He can also be found under the guise of Kent Montana creator/humorist Lionel Fenn, as well as Timothy Boggs, author of expansion novels regarding the *Hercules* TV saga. He lives in New Jersey with his wife, author and Gila Queen's Guide to Markets/Horror Writers Association newsletter editor, Kathryn Ptacek.

A winner of the Nebula Award, the British Lifetime Achievement Award, the Bram Stoker's Lifetime Achievement Award from the Horror Writers Association, World Horror Grand Master Award, the World Fantasy Award and more.

Charles L. Grant passed away on September 15, 2006.

MORE MODERN MYTHMAKERS: You were the recipient of the International Horror Guild's Living Legend Award. What does that award mean to you?

CHARLES L. GRANT: I think it means I must be ready to die (laughs). I received three of them in two years. I don't know what to say. It is really nice to have. I'm pleased that they thought about me, whoever voted for these things. I'm not old enough for that kind of thing. I'm only 60. This is the kind of award you get when you are in your 70s and 80s. I'm not done yet. Because of what ails me, it takes me considerably longer to write than it used to.

MMM: For *Night Song*, did you have to research the occult, or did you just create mythology according to what the plot required?

GRANT: (laughs). Ed Bryant always says, "I never do research, I just make it up." Almost, but not quite true. I wanted to do a zombie novel based on real zombies, not the George Romero kind of zombies. I did some research to make sure that my idea of zombies wasn't all taken from the movies.

MMM: What came first for *Symphony*, the plotline, or the personification of the apocalypse?

GRANT: The idea came first. It was the only commercial idea I had in my whole life, and it flopped. I wanted to do four books each based on the Four Horseman. I wanted each of the Four Horseman to be different than anyone has ever thought of them before. That is why you got a woman, a kid, a guy who looks remarkably like Willie Nelson and an old black woman. I didn't want flowing robes or literally riding horses, or at least not until the end. I pitched that idea to my editor, who loved it, and the publisher loved it. It took me about five years to write the series.

MMM: Is Ethan Proctor from the *Black Oak* series based on a real person specifically debunking the supernatural?

GRANT: The idea was I could do *The X-Files* better than *The X-Files*. Unlike *The X-Files*, I wouldn't be making it up as I went along. This was the idea of a British editor who asked my agent if I ever thought about doing an *X-Files* type series. And I hadn't at the time. As soon as it was mentioned, I thought I could do that; I could have fun and do all kinds of different things.

I gave the British editor my proposal and that SOB turned it down. But my editor at ROC picked it up. I projected a 12 or 13 book series with one whole story that would take three or four novels to tell, just like a TV show. I based it on that story arc business. Plus, one story that would begin and end in each book.

I loved it and had a great time. I had not gotten such mail on any of my books or my entire career—when ROC killed it halfway through. I'm hoping to get it done somehow. The sixth book is halfway done, it wouldn't take much to get that finished. I don't outline, I never did. But I set things up for each book in the series. It will probably have to be a small press that is willing to take a chance on it, because the major publishers won't pick it up.

MMM: In the *X-Files* book, *Goblins,* were the supporting characters and Scully's interaction with them your own creation or was that something specified by Chris Carter?

GRANT: Everything in those books, except Scully and Mulder are mine. Carter kept his hands off, except to fire me. He didn't like them.

MMM: TV shows don't generally use much profanity, were you comfortable adding that element to *Goblins*? Were there any concerns from Chris Carter or the Fox Network because of that?

GRANT: The copy editor said, 'Mulder wouldn't say that.' I wrote a note back and said, 'look at the show, he's swearing all the time.' According to Chris Carter I didn't get Mulder and Scully right. Carter said the two books (*Goblins* and W*hirlwind*) were 'noir'; which is dark, and he said *The X-Files* wasn't."

MMM: What would you consider your favorite; the most perfect Charles Grant book and why?

GRANT: There is none. I'm not satisfied with anything that I have done. I don't read them when they come out because I'm not going to like them. The only thing I do is after they are published, I check the beginning to see if they got the beginning right, and to make sure they haven't screwed up the ending. By the time the book is out of our house, I don't ever want to see it again (laughs). I'll just read a paragraph and say, "that's awful, why did I write it that way?"

MMM: What was the inspiration for *Jackals*?

GRANT: One day I was actually watching PBS. I was surfing the channels and I happened to hit upon this show about lions and hyenas. I caught this bit where the pride (lions) was hanging on the edge of this herd of impalas. The lead hyena is a female, it is a matriarchy. The lions had marked their territory. She would put her mark on top of the lion's mark. Like "nanana." One lion would come back and mark it again. And she'd do it all over again. She was really pissing the lions off. There seems to be some confusion here between lions and hyenas, it's not clear to me. I think you meant to say "hyena" in several places instead of "lion."

All of the sudden, the impalas scattered. Out of this herd, comes this huge male lion in full charge and he goes right for that hyena, and she doesn't get very far. It was one bite, and she was dead.

It was amazing. I was in my animal period, I just finished *Raven*, I was casting about for something else, and that image stuck in my mind. I didn't like the idea of hyenas, but I liked jackals. I thought I'll change the hyenas to jackals and make the jackals human and my hero was the lion. I even used the phrase "charging out of the herd."

MMM: Last words?

GRANT: There you go again, I'm not dead yet (laughs). I wish more people would buy my books, so I can keep on writing. It's kind of doubtful these days. My goal has always been the same since the day I started out, which is not to scare anyone but to make them really, really nervous. Lifetime achievement awards or not, they are going to have to kill me to stop me from writing (laughs).

"The 'theme song' from Swan Lake *is much beloved by horror fans—it's what they play in the opening for* The Mummy *(the Boris Karloff version) and* Dracula *(the Bela Lugosi version). I suppose that's fitting for a ballet whose original version featured the double suicide of the main characters"*

—Nancy Holder

DAUGHTER OF THE BLOOD
NANCY HOLDER

NEW YORK TIMES bestselling author Nancy Holder was born in Palo Alto, California, and her family settled for a time in Walnut Creek. Her father, who taught at Stanford, joined the Navy, and the family traveled throughout California, and lived in Japan for three years. When she was sixteen, she dropped out of high school to become a ballet dancer in Cologne, Germany, and later relocated to Frankfurt am Main.

Eventually, she returned to California and graduated from the University of California in San Diego with a degree in Communications. Soon after, she began to write; her first sale was a young adult romance novel titled *Teach Me to Love*. She currently lives in Port Townsend, Washington with her Corgi, Tater.

Nancy's work has appeared on the bestseller lists of *The New York Times*, *USA Today*, The *LA Times*, amazon.com,

Locus and others. Seven time winner the Bram Stoker Awards from the Horror Writers Association including Lifetime Achievement, she was named the 2019 Faust Grandmaster by the International Association of Media Tie-In Writers, and received a YA Pioneer Award from RT Booksellers. She is a Baker Street Irregular ("Beryl Garcia") and is very active in the world of Sherlock Holmes. She wrote the online storytelling game *The Unsolved Cases of Sherlock Holmes* for Storium™ and co-edited *Sherlock Holmes of Baking Street* with Margie Deck, which will be out in June 2021 from Belanger Books. She lectures and writes essays, articles, and short fiction about Holmes. She was a guest at Australia's SupaNova conventions in Melbourne and the Gold Coast in 2019.

She has sold approximately nine dozen book-length projects, many of them set in the *Teen Wolf, Buffy the Vampire Slayer*, and *Angel* universes. She has also novelized the films *Wonder Woman, Crimson Peak,* and *Ghostbusters. Wicked*, her *New York Times* bestselling series for Simon and Schuster, was co-authored with former Maui Writers Retreat student, Debbie Viguié. She has written young adult and adult dark fantasy, horror, mysteries, science fiction, and romance; and has written under many house names including Carolyn Keene, writing Nancy Drew.

She served on the faculty of the University of Southern Maine's Stonecoast MFA in Creative Writing for fourteen years, and also taught in the literature department at the University of California at San Diego.

She has edited or co-edited six anthologies. Her anthology *Outsiders*, co-edited with Nancy Kilpatrick, was nominated for the Bram Stoker Award in 2005.

Her other deep interest is Mary Shelley. She is the writer in the *Mary Shelley Presents* graphic novel/comic book series from Kymera Press, which was nominated for a 2020 Bram Stoker Award. She recently sold "Catfather," about the Frankenstein Creature's cat. She also writes and edits pulp fiction and comics for Moonstone Books, where her work centers on the Domino Lady; her daughter Domino Patrick (co-created with Joe Gentile); Kolchak the Night Stalker; the Green Hornet; and Johhny Fade (co-created with Alan Philipson). Her website is www.nancyholder.com.

MORE MODERN MYTHMAKERS: What are some of your favorite vampire books and movies?

NANCY HOLDER:
   Books: I'll go for some classics: the aforementioned *Vampire Tapestry;* Chelsea Quinn Yarbro's books about the Count St. Germain; the original *Dracula; Let the Right One In; I am Legend; Interview with the Vampire, Salem's Lot, Fevre Dream.* I am looking forward to Grady Hendrix's *The Southern Book Club's Guide to Slaying Vampires,* which is on my TBR (To Be Read) stack.
   Some movies: Near *Dark, The Lost Boys, Let the Right One In; The Hunger;* Coppola's *Dracula* because it is just so bombastic and insane; *Isle of the Dead. Isle of the Dead* was produced by one of my very favorite horror auteurs, Val Lewton. His protégé, Robert Wise, directed my favorite horror film of all time, which is not a vampire movie: *The Haunting* (1963 version). I adore the work of Alfonso Cuarón, Pedro Almodovar, and Guillermo del Toro, not all of it vampiric, although *Cronos* was cool, especially for a first effort. Right now I'm working on a short story for an Australian Dracula anthology; my story concerns Japanese ghosts so I rewatched *Kwaidan,* an amazing film. The part I'm concentrating on is "Hoichi the Earless." The restless ghosts in that creepy, gorgeous section are essentially vampires.

MMM: Why do you think vampire books and movies are so popular? Did this trend boost the sales of your *Buffy* books?
HOLDER: Vampire books and movies are always popular.

I remember the Little Bookshop of Horrors in Denver. They had a bay labeled "New Books" and a bay labeled "Vampires." This was forever ago. I have gotten recent offers to write more *Buffy* books.

MMM: You presented Chelsea Quinn Yarbo with the Lifetime Achievement Award in June 2009 at the Bram Stoker Award ceremony. What was it like giving one of your idols such a prestigious honor?

HOLDER: Giving Chelsea Quinn Yarbo that award was definitely one of the highlights of my career. I started reading her before I got published. I was so exhausted when I got the Stokers—deadlines, parental responsibilities—that I got up to have breakfast with a friend, then went to bed for hours. I felt a bit disoriented when I came downstairs for the banquet, and I started to worry about making a muddle of it. Quinn and I sat together at the banquet and I realized that this wasn't about me. This was for Quinn. I didn't have a prepared speech. And I was so overcome at the podium that I doubt I would have been able to say it properly anyway. I admire Chelsea Quinn Yarbo so deeply. She is one of our treasures. I am so, so honored to know her.

MMM: The Bram Stoker Awards are just about the highest honors a horror writer can get. How does it feel to be a seven-time winner?

HOLDER: It's wonderful. I have all my little houses populated with a village of miniature monsters, scary trees, and tombstones. I'd like to win some more. You can't have enough Bram Stokers.

MMM: How do you maintain an active fascination for horror?

HOLDER: I think it is very important to stay connected to other horror writers and readers. The easiest way to do this is to join the Horror Writers Association—go to horror.org. I've served as vice-president, a member of the board, and a Bram Stoker Award juror for the HWA, and all of them were (and are) extremely rewarding experiences. HWA offers health insurance, camaraderie, and a mentorship program. In 2020, with the arrival of Zoom meetings, it's easy to stay in touch with fellow HWA and other horror folks. Lots of horror people meet up on Facebook as well. Many writers are 1) shy and 2) introverted, but it's important to connect.

Through the horror community, I stay current on new books and movies. I haven't been watching *What We Do in the Shadows,* for example, but I'm dying to.

MMM: As a former ballet dancer in Germany, I was wondering if you saw the movie *Black Swan*? If so, what are your thoughts on the film?

HOLDER: I did see *Black Swan* and I loved it. The controversy over Natalie Portman's ballet double was fascinating, and added to the bombast. The pressure of being perfect takes its toll on most dancers, and the accumulated physical damage later in life is something dancers should be prepared for. In ballet classes, teachers exhort their students toward regal postures by saying, "Long necks for *Swan Lake*." I used to imagine someone chopping off my head. Obviously, I was not meant for the stage. But I love to exercise—I'm a Jazzercise fanatic—and I love to think of my body as a piece of equipment.

The 'theme song' from *Swan Lake* is much beloved by horror fans—it's what they play in the opening for *The Mummy* (the Boris Karloff version) and *Dracula* (the Bela Lugosi version). I suppose that's fitting for a ballet whose original version featured the double suicide of the main characters.

MMM: Of your collected work, which book was the easiest to write and which one was the most difficult and why?

HOLDER: One of the books that I loved writing, which therefore made it easy, is the novelization of *Crimson Peak*. I admire Guillermo del Toro so much. I read and watched interviews with him and discovered (to my delight) that many of his influences dovetail with my own: films such as Cousteau's *Beauty and the Beast* and the 1931 *Frankenstein*, and books such as *The Vampire Tapestry* by Suzy McKee Charnas. I was allowed to add a lot to that book, and it was a loving tribute to GdT as well as to Gothic fiction. It doesn't hurt that he loves to ride the Haunted Mansion at Disneyland and I'm a Disney kid.

The most difficult is a book I won't name. It was sold on an outline and sample writing for a lot of money, and as soon as the ink dried on the contract, my editor demanded that I completely alter my direction from what I had sold to them. I was shocked, but I allowed myself to be bullied because of the money, and the result was—of course—mediocre. It is so hard to know when to bend and when to say no. There are times when it is prudent to acquiesce, but this was not one of them.

MMM: You've written dozens of books set in the *Buffy the Vampire Slayer, Angel, Sabrina the Teenage Witch,* and *Smallville* universes. How do you make their universe your own?

HOLDER:I'm the kind of person who becomes intensely attracted to whatever I'm interested in. The only universe I wasn't already a fan of before I was offered the gig was *Saving Grace*. My agent had lunch with the acquiring editor, who asked if I liked the show. I watched the first season and my jaw dropped. I was born to watch *Saving*

Grace, just as I was born to watch *Buffy*. I couldn't get enough of *Saving Grace*. I wrote an article about this for *The Cult TV Book,* edited by Stacey Abbott. I have to love the show I'm working on so much that *I* stop mattering. I try to serve as a real scribe, enhancing the vision of the show creator or creators. It's not my job to interpret; it's my job to present. Sometimes that makes it a little difficult if I disagree with the direction the show is taking. But it's not my business to correct that. It's my business to reflect on it.

Right now I'm working on *Kolchak the Night Stalker,* with enough room to do some interpretation, so that's nice. I've also novelized a few movies. As I mentioned, my favorite movie experience was working on *Crimson Peak.* I adore Guillermo del Toro.

MMM: How did *Crimson Peak* come about?

HOLDER: I got hired by Titan to novelize Guillermo del Toro's film for *Legendary.* I drove up to the lot to watch a screening with a bunch of marketing executives. I had printed the script out and annotated it with a color-coded system of sticky notes, in an extremely complicated charting system that was basically organized that way to keep track of the movie's point of view. I wound up adding my own invented point of view as well. But when we started to watch the movie, all the lights went out and it was extremely dark, and I realized I was going to have to take notes in real time. This was my only chance to watch the film. So I flipped the entire script over and scribbled notes on the backsides of all my pages. I was in a sweat. When something violent happened on the screen, one of the execs shouted, "Oh, no!" I grinned to myself—*gotcha!*—and kept scribbling.

MMM: When you are writing dialogue for your characters how do you keep it from running too long or too short?

HOLDER: Working on tie-in material, I read tons of scripts, and I think that's rubbed off on me. Right now I'm watching lots of noir films with my writing partner Alan Philipson while we work on *Johnny Fade in Deadtown*. I absolutely love the snappy, sexy cadence of noir. The characters say a lot by not saying much. Silence is a powerful form of speech.

MMM: If you could be a monster, what monster would you be and why?

HOLDER: I don't know if this counts, but I would be a queen of dark magic. I'd get the best spells and the best clothes that way. And I'd look great! But if I have to pick a classic monster, I'd probably be a vampire, for pretty much the same reasons. I've survived in publishing for a long time, so I've been acquainted with a few vampires (SNAP!) and I'd know my way around the bloodsucking community right off the bat (sorry!).

MMM: How can a writer boost their sales when their books are in a slump?

HOLDER: It's important to keep a presence on social media and to stay actively known as a horror writer. Volunteering to be on an award jury, mentioning new films and books online; blogging—staying in the mix. It's important to present yourself as a writer, and not simply as someone flogging books. It's also important not to apologize for your (perceived) lack of success. We're all in this together, and every voice in horror has something to say. Don't count yourself out. Don't be overly humble. Try not to compete. You are a creative person with your own quirky take on the world—and worlds beyond.

MMM: You have written over a hundred books. Have you ever suffered from writer's block?

HOLDER: I've suffered from panic, exhaustion, and confusion. I think those situations make for writer's block. My life is a lot more settled now and I take on fewer projects, but I still overschedule and juggle. And I start skipping other things I want to do, such as seriously pursuing my yoga studies.

MMM: You have written a number of collaborations. What is the key to successfully writing a novel together?

HOLDER: As long as you have a co-author who is equally dedicated to making the book as good as it can be, your collaboration will work. The trick is to establish a system. This is mine: you get the work from the other guy, edit it, add to it, and turn it back to your partner. What they get back is what exists now. The old drafts are gone. I'm working with Alan Philipson, who has written tons of books under house names, and we are doing great. We have created a new pulp character named Johnny Fade. I still remember sitting in Melanie Tem's cabin up among the aspens, working together, away from everything. So special. I miss her dearly.

MMM: You have written young adult horror. How would you define young adult horror? What is the difference between it and grown-up horror?

HOLDER: Young adult horror pulls some punches when it comes to the gore factor and subject matter. Also, how dark you can go. I do pull back on the throttle. There is no such thing as grown-up horror. Fear is an atavistic emotion. Horror grabs the little child in us as surely as Pennywise grabbed George Denbrough.

I take that back. There *is* such a thing as grown-up horror. When I think of horrible, real things that could and have happened, I wish them on myself instead of my loved ones. That's terrifying, but it's grown-up.

MMM: What's the hardest part of being a professional writer?

HOLDER: Practically, making a living. Juggling, making all of your life work. Artistically, staying fresh and keeping the momentum going. Lawrence Kasdan (screenwriter of *Dreamcatchers, The Bodyguard, Star Wars 5: Empire Strikes Back, Body Heat,* etc.) said, "Being a writer is like having homework for the rest of your life." This is accurate. If you can bear that, you can be a writer. I love being a writer. When I get into the flow, there's nothing like it on earth. It's yoga with words.

MMM: Last words?

HOLDER: Read and write what you love. Watch and rewatch what you love. Life is short. Sink your teeth into your passions.

"I was quite jealous of the authors writing tales for the Hellbound Hearts book I'd just been editing . . . Thankfully Clive gave his blessing and it paid off, but yes it could all have gone horribly wrong"

—Paul Kane

VOICES IN THE DARK
PAUL KANE

BY MICHAEL MCCARTY & HOLLY ZALDIVAR

PAUL KANE IS the award-winning, #1 bestselling author and editor of over a hundred books—including the *Hooded Man* trilogy, *The Naked Eye,* and *Wonderland* (a Shirley Jackson Award finalist). He has been a Guest at many conventions, as well as being a panelist at FantasyCon and the World Fantasy Convention, and a fiction judge at the Sci-Fi London festival.

A former British Fantasy Society Special Publications Editor, he is currently serving as co-chair for the UK chapter of The Horror Writers Association. His work has been optioned and adapted for the big and small screen, including for US network primetime television, and his novelette 'Men of the Cloth' has just been turned into a feature by Loose Canon/Hydra Films, starring Barbara Crampton (*Re-Animator, You're Next*): *Sacrifice,* released by Epic Pictures/101 Films. His audio work includes the full cast drama adaptation of *The Hellbound Heart* for Bafflegab, starring Tom Meeten (*The Ghoul*), Neve McIntosh (*Doctor Who*) and Alice Lowe (*Prevenge*), and the *Robin of Sherwood* adventure *The Red Lord* for Spiteful Puppet/ITV narrated by Ian Ogilvy (*Return of the Saint*). Paul's latest novels include the award-winning hit *Sherlock Holmes & the Servants of Hell*, *Before* (an Amazon Top 5 dark fantasy bestseller), and *Arcana*. In addition, he writes thrillers for HQ/HarperCollins as PL Kane, the first of which, *Her Last Secret* and *Her Husband's Grave* (a recent sellout on both Amazon and Waterstones), came out in 2020. Paul lives in Derbyshire, UK, with his wife Marie O'Regan and his family.

Find out more at his site www.shadow-writer.co.uk

MORE MODERN MYTHMAKERS: *Sherlock Holmes and the Servants of Hell* thrust super sleuth Sherlock Holmes and his ever-faithful companion Dr. John Watson into Clive Barker's *Hellraiser* universe. Was this a difficult task to achieve, taking two polar worlds and combining them together? Do you see any sequels in the future?

PAUL KANE: It was incredibly daunting, as you run the risk of upsetting two massive fan bases at the same time. Because I'm a huge fan of both franchises, I wanted to do them both justice. From most of the feedback I got, I seem to have done that, which is nice. And a lot of people tell me it's either their favorite book or favorite crossover/mashup, which is incredibly gratifying. As with anything else, it was a case of me thinking to myself 'what's not out there already that I'd like to read myself?' It was how the *Hellraiser Films and Their Legacy* came about, there just wasn't a book at the time covering all the movies and comics or whatever, so I figured I'd write one.

As for combining the two universes, I've told this story before quite a few times, but I grew up reading both Clive's work and the Holmes adventures, plus watching the *Hellraiser* movies and the Granada TV show with Jeremy Brett as Holmes. Somewhere in my head these two had merged together anyway at an early age, so that had stayed with me. If you think about it, the Holmes era is ripe for horror anyway—you've got Jack the Ripper running around, Dracula out around that time, and indeed one of my all-time favorite Holmes adventures I'd classify as horror: *The Hound of the Baskervilles*. Indeed, there was a plan originally to have a segment of *Hellraiser: Bloodline* set in Victorian times, so it all just made perfect sense to me. The Cenobites have been around forever, so why not back then? That was one of the things I adored about the old Epic *Hellraiser* comics, that they had different historical settings. I recall one which took place in Medieval Times, for example. Similarly, when my better half, Marie O'Regan, and I edited the anthology of *Hellraiser*-related stories *Hellbound Hearts*, there were tales from different periods in history in that too: Sarah Pinborough wrote us a cracking story inspired by fairy tales for instance called 'The Confessor's Tale.'

I'd just started writing Sherlock Holmes horror stories myself—my first was 'The Greatest Mystery' in *Gaslight Arcanum*, in which Holmes confronts Death—so putting him in the *Hellraising* world Clive Barker had created just seemed like a no-brainer to me. And I was quite jealous of the authors writing tales for the *Hellbound Hearts* book I'd just been editing . . . Thankfully Clive gave his blessing and it paid off, but yes it could all have gone horribly wrong.

As for a sequel, there's a lot going on in the *Hellraiser* universe at the moment with the reboot and the TV show, so there are no plans at present. But never say never!

MMM: You are no stranger to horror fiction. Would you mind explaining a bit about the fiction you write? How do you approach the genre?

KANE: I started off writing horror, but I've actually written a bit of everything in my time—from comedy to thrillers, most recently the PL Kane novels for HQ/HarperCollins: *Her Last Secret* and *Her Husband's Grave*. My *Hooded Man* novels are also classed as SF technically, and my short stories cover everything from Surrealism to Slipstream. There are even elements of Steampunk in *Servants*, which we've just been talking about. So, yeah, all kinds of subjects and genres. But I did start my career writing just horror for small press magazines. I was heavily influenced by books from the '70s and '80s boom, an avid reader of authors like Clive, James Herbert, Anne Rice, Stephen King . . . But again, I was reading all kinds of fiction back then, from Frank Herbert to Colin Dexter and Tolkien, although it was the darker stuff I gravitated towards when I first began putting pen to paper or bashing away on my mum's old typewriter.

The thing I love about horror is that it's so versatile, you can splice it with any other genre. You can have an SF-horror, an historical-horror, a horror-fantasy—like my book *Arcana*, which deals with magic in an alternate reality—or a crime-horror like the first serious novel I ever wrote, *The Gemini Factor*, which just came out in an anniversary edition. It's constantly re-inventing itself, which keeps things fresh and interesting for me as both a reader and a writer. So, I approach it from the perspective of writing something that interests me or allows me to get things off my chest—which horror, like all the imaginative genres, lets you do indirectly. My novel *Before*, for example, gave me scope to write about human beings and what we're doing here on this planet, why things are going wrong and how we can fix them, whilst at the same time presenting a chase story where a supernatural power is pursuing a man and woman for reasons, we're not privy to at the start. That's an exciting prospect for a writer.

The kind of horror I write also depends on the story I'm tackling. The Controllers mythos are a good example of two extremes, in that I can write broadly about cosmic horror for one story involving them, then in the next one it might be an intimate character study. I like to think I write well-rounded characters in situations that are beyond the norm, grounding them first and then exposing them to something outside of their experience. Or indeed ours. In the most recent collection, *The Naked Eye* from Encyclopocalypse, there's a tale called "The Cursed" which was about a character who messed his life up by cursing a relationship. That gave me room to comment on the decisions we make in the spur of the moment, how we screw things up and look back at the mistakes. But a few stories later, you then have a horror superhero tale with my popular character Mortis-Man, so I like to vary things and keep people on their toes.

MMM: What was the underlying motivation for *Darkness & Shadows*?

KANE: Basically, to gather together all of my "Order of the Shadows" stories that I've been writing since the '90s. One of the very first horror shorts I wrote was "Shadow Writer" which my website is still named after, but I did a few more featuring them after this—and had ideas for a couple more, which ended up being the brand-new stories in the book. I'd also been looking for a way to reprint a rare short novel of mine from 2010 that was first published by Thunderstorm Books as a limited hardback and trade paperback, *Of Darkness and Light*. There are themes in that one which parallel the stuff in the "Order . . . " mythos, coming at it from a slightly different angle. So, I had the idea of putting both of these together, to come up with . . . *Darkness & Shadows*.

I'd worked with the Sinister Horror Company when they brought out my *Death* collection a few years ago, so I approached Justin again to see if he'd be interested, and thankfully he was! We timed it well, too, because at the same time Distant Grey Gaming were in talks with me about doing a roleplaying game based around 'Shadow Writer' so it all fit together quite nicely. I also had an ulterior motive in mind because at some point, I want to cross over The Controllers and The Order in a longer story, either a novella or short novel. Luna Press had already gathered together all of my Controllers tales, so now if people want to get a head start on both mythos they can read *The Controllers* and *Darkness & Shadows* first.

MMM: What is it about ghosts that attracts your attention? Do you believe ghosts really exist?

KANE: Oh, *absolutely* I believe! I've experienced strange things in that area myself and visited quite a number of haunted places, such as Annesley Hall, where I spent one Halloween, and Rowtor Rocks. The most haunted I think was Craig Y Nos Castle in Wales which Marie and I visited a couple of times back when we were just friends, both times for book launches. They were doing things like ghost hunts and table tipping, but I was staying on my own in a place called The Nurses' Lodgings. All night long there were 'people' walking up and down the corridors outside my room, and voices chattering away, but when you opened the door, there'd be nobody there.

It's experiences like this that fuel stories like "Creakers" and "Presence,' which is being turned into a short movie at the moment. There are more things in Heaven and Earth and all that. And I think it's quite a comforting thing to think sometimes that we go on, in whatever form, after we die. It wasn't until I checked that I found I had enough stories in this vein to put together the collection *Ghosts* back in 2013, the hardback of which came with the DVD of the short movie 'Wind Chimes.' That, again, was inspired by a visit to a children's graveyard with a friend. I mean, I didn't know that's where we were going; one minute we were walking through a park and then suddenly there were all these tiny little grave-stones and crosses, with wind chimes hanging in the trees. The way they were tinkling sounded very much like children's voices and so the germ of the idea for that one was created.

MMM: I'm a big fan of *Voices in the Dark: Interviews with Horror, Writers, Directors & Actors* (co-written with Marie O'Regan). If you were interviewing Paul Kane for that book, what question would you ask yourself?

KANE: Well, thanks very much! Delighted that you liked it. Marie and I enjoyed putting that one together. We were basically interviewing a lot of genre names for magazine articles, so we thought to ourselves why not compile them and put in new material as well? It made for a very unique book I think, featuring the likes of Neil Gaiman, Clive Barker, Christa Campbell, Mick Garris, Stuart Gordon . . .

If I was interviewing that scoundrel 'Paul Kane'? Hmm . . . I'd probably ask what his deepest, darkest secret was. But that doesn't necessarily mean he'd answer! More seriously, I'd ask if he had anything to tell the younger version of himself just setting out on this long road 25 years ago? And the answer to that would be to just hang in there and keep the faith. Things are going to go wrong, but then that's the nature of the business—and indeed life itself. Always have faith that it happened for the best of reasons, though, and something better will come along. It's a hard life being a writer sometimes, but the rewards can be enormous; I'm not just talking financial here, but other things. One person emailed me a few years ago to thank me because they're disabled and housebound, so my stories were the only way they could be transported out of the house via their imagination. That's hugely gratifying to me, especially as I had a father who was in the same situation towards the end of his life. He got me into horror, so in a funny sort of way things came full circle.

MMM: Did you have any interviews that you wanted to do for *Voices in the Dark* that didn't happen or pan out. Can you name names?

KANE: Oh, there were a few. The ones that stand out, who couldn't take part because of time or whatever, were Bruce Campbell—I absolutely adore his work, and the *Evil Dead* franchise in particular—and M. Night Shyamalan. Marie and I are both massive fans of films like *The Sixth Sense* and *Unbreakable*. We were also scheduled to interview Stan Winston, which would have been amazing, but of course sadly he passed away before we could meet up with him. Finally, there was HR Giger, who is one of my favorite artists. I was invited over to Switzerland a couple of times to interview him prior to the first book coming out but didn't have the spare cash to go at the time—and then of course he passed away too. It's one of my biggest regrets. He would have been part of a *Voices II* if we'd managed to get that off the ground, but it wasn't to be. I'd love to have chatted to the man who designed the *Alien*! That would have been a dream come true!

MMM: Why did you decide to name your novella *Sleeper(s)* instead of just *Sleepers*?

KANE: Anyone who's aware of what *Sleeper(s)* is about, or what it's based on, will know the answer to that one immediately. Not only are there sleepers, plural, people being controlled by a possible alien force, willing to attack when it feels threatened, but there's also a woman at the center of the plague. My version of Sleeping Beauty, because at the end of the day this is one of my modern horror fairy tales reworkings, like *Red*. She's the Sleeper, singular, at the core of both the outbreak and the story. So, the title refers to both really.

I gathered together all of these stories in a collection called *Kane's Scary Tales Vol. 1* a couple of years ago, which also contained *Snow* and a new novelette called *Giants*. Work's already begun on a second collection—which might take a while, as the first was about 15 years in the making—but you can read the first of those in my latest collection mentioned earlier, *The Naked Eye*. That's a reworking of Hansel and Gretel called 'Crumbs,' which has a nod to Ray Harryhausen's work towards the end.

MMM: In the wake of the post Covid-19 pandemic, have your thoughts on your books *The Rot* and *Sleeper(s)* changed any or not?

KANE: I think anyone who's written post-apocalyptic fiction in the past would have looked at events during 2020 and 2021 and thought 'this is a bit too close to what we've been imagining for comfort.' Marie and I were down in London just before the first lockdown—we live in Derbyshire in the Midlands—and we only just got out of the city in time. One of our friends said to me before we left, 'It's just like one of your novels, Paul,' to which I replied, 'You'd better hope not, they never end well!'

I mean, the stories—at least the ones I wrote—were meant as warnings and they're still warnings, like any other PA (Post Apocalyptic) tale. *The Terminator* is essentially a warning about creating an AI that might suddenly turn around and try and wipe out the human race. And as bad as things have been globally, they haven't been on the scale of the A-B Virus from the Afterblight Chronicles, which *Hooded Man* belongs to, or *The Rot* or even *Sleeper(s)*; one Hollywood producer described that, quite accurately, as *Inception* meets *Outbreak*, although I'd argue—as Dr

Strauss comments himself—there's a healthy dose of *The Midwich Cuckoos* in there too. I haven't been writing any PA pieces during the pandemic or lockdown, if that's what you're asking, for obvious reasons. Luckily, it's all been about crime-thriller fiction with my PL Kane books. But the state of the world has certainly been throwing up ideas for future PA stories. I don't think you can look at all this and *not* get ideas as a writer for PA tales, but the time's probably not right yet to sell them. Maybe when all this has been behind us a while . . .

MMM: Boarding schools are the setting of several British horror novels. Why are speculative fiction writers in the UK fascinated with finishing schools?

KANE: I'm not sure I'm the right person to answer that really, as I didn't go to one. I went to a regular public school and didn't stay over. I'm not aware personally of a huge amount of horror novels that focus on those; I guess the Harry Potters are technically horror . . . But I can't really speak for any of the people who've written them, though at a push I'd say they're a place where you're separated from home and all you know. They're places where you're forced to fend for yourself, where there's a kind of *Lord of the Flies* mentality I suppose.

My stablemate at Abaddon, Scott Andrews, actually set his *Afterblight* books at a boarding school—and his first book has just been adapted into the movie *School's Out Forever*. So, he'd probably be a better person to ask about what inspired that. As a side note, Scott and I ended up crossing our characters over quite a bit—with my version of Robin Hood cropping up in his stuff, and his King of England in mine. We had such fun working all that out, I do remember that, and coming up with nasty threats for our heroes to face.

MMM: What is the best advice another writer has ever given you?

KANE: That would probably be from Simon Clark, author of books like *King Blood* and *Vampyrrhic*. I first met Simon at one of the earliest writer get-togethers I attended in Sheffield, one of the now infamous Terror Scribes gatherings organized by John B. Ford. I was just starting out and Simon was writing the kind of fiction I wanted to pen, for places like Hodder & Stoughton and Cemetery Dance. I remember Simon saying, "Just keep your head down and get on with the work. It's easy to get distracted, but it's all about doing good work. And then one day you'll look back and see just how far you've come." Well, over 100 publications later and with a #1 bestselling author credit to my name, I can definitely say he was right.

I'm also happy to report that Simon became one of my best friends in the business, he's very generously introduced a couple of my collections and we've even collaborated on a book called *Beneath the Surface*. So, it's nice when the people who give you advice stay with you on the path and continue to help you along.

MMM: If you could be a monster, which monster would you be and why?

KANE: If we're taking the Cenobites and the *Nightbreed* as read, some of my favorite and some of the most powerful monsters of all time, then I'd have to say the alien in the Alien movies. It's virtually indestructible and you don't dare kill it because its blood is acid! Of course, there's not a lot going on in the brain department apart from survival or following orders from the Alien Queen, so I'm not sure how satisfying that would be . . .

As another aside, this gives me the perfect opportunity to mention my short novel *The Storm* from PS Publishing which came out in 2020. That's basically my love letter to monster movies and books, from smaller creatures to the bigger ones that can swallow you whole. Some of my own personal favorites I created are in there, so if anyone is a fan of monsters then that one is definitely for you!

MMM: Do you think humor and horror work well? Why or why not?

KANE: As someone who's written comedy horror, I'd have to say a big fat yes! Back in the day all of my humorous horror fiction—what one of my writing students used to call 'Horredy' back when I was teaching classes—was collected in *Funny Bones*. Pieces like 'Dracula in Love' and 'The Bones Brothers.' Then I had a collection out called *The Adventures of Dalton Quayle*, featuring my titular detective who investigates the supernatural. All of his most popular capers were in there from 'Master of the White Worms' to 'Temple of Deadly Danger' and more.

I grew up loving horror comedies myself, like *Evil Dead II* and *House*, so that influence has again been there a long time. They just go hand-in-hand really because of the outlandish situation's horror lends itself to. You could take any horror premise and make a comedy out of it, like they've done with films such as *Dracula: Dead and Loving It* and the *Scary Movie* series. What can be terrifying under certain circumstances or with the right direction, can be hilarious if given a comedic tweak.

MMM: Last words?

KANE: Just to say how very grateful I am that people keep buying my books, watching my films, or listening to the audios. It's the reason we sit down every day and do this. The writing community, especially in the field of horror, is incredibly supportive as well—so I'll say a thank you to everyone who's a part of that.

"I have a great nostalgic love for Halloween. When I was a kid it was an all-month event. Me, my brother, and our friends planned it meticulously; the decorations, the costumes, the Trick-or-Treat route."

—Ronald Kelly

DARK DIXIE
RONALD KELLY

IN HIS ANTHOLOGY, *Borderlands 3*, Thomas F. Monteleone said this considering Ronald Kelly and his particular brand of fiction . . .

"There is a sub-genre that seems to have come to life on its own—a kind of spontaneous generation once ascribed to maggots on dead meat, or that coiling swirl of dust balls in the corner of an abandoned house. It's called Southern Horror, and it's marked largely by a preying upon the natural urban paranoia of the rest of us, i.e., those of us who don't live in places called "vales" or "corners" or "hollows." Ronald Kelly writes the stuff, and it's marked by a strong regional flavor, a familiarity with custom and superstition, and a style that can't be faked."

From the mid-1980s to the mid-1990s, Kelly made a name for himself in the horror fiction community writing what he now coins as "Southern-Fried Horror," first in the small press and, later, as an author for Zebra Books. Kelly's unique appeal? Traditional storytelling that sprang from family history and ghost stories, deep roots to a blue collar/rural farming background, and locales that weren't commonly explored at that time. Kelly's tales encompassed every state of the American South, most notably his home territory of Tennessee. For the six years he wrote for Zebra, Kelly penned such memorable novels as *Fear*, *Blood Kin*, *Hindsight*, *Moon of the Werewolf*, *Pitfall*, *Something Out There*, *Father's Little Helper*, *Haunt of Southern-Fried Fear* and *The Possession*. His audiobook, *Dark Dixie,* was even nominated for a Grammy Award in 1992.

When the bottom dropped out of mass market publishing in the mid-90s and Zebra closed down their horror line, Kelly took a ten-year hiatus from writing in the genre. For the next decade, he returned to the blue collar factories, raised a family, and avoided dark fiction like the plague. He returned in 2006, and continued writing Southern-fried horror like he had never stopped. To date, he has fifteen novels and twelve short fiction collections to his credit.

Kelly currently lives in the rural community of Brush Creek, Tennessee, with his wife, Joyce, and his passel of young'uns.

MORE MODERN MYTHMAKERS:How many editor's desks did *Hindsight* hit before ending at Zebra Books? Were you surprised that Kensington Publishing picked it up? What did they like best about the manuscript?

RONALD KELLY: My agent at the time, the Scott Meredith Agency, had *Hindsight*—which was originally titled *The Tobacco Barn*—for two and a half years before it sold. He must have submitted it to every publisher in the alphabet, because it finally ended up at Zebra. I must say that I was stunned when my agent called me at work and told me that Kensington had made an offer for it. After writing short fiction for the small press for years, actually selling a novel to a major mass market was a huge step for me. They seemed taken by my style of rural, Southern horror, which was something that wasn't commonly explored in the genre at that time. I was both pleased and a bit apprehensive. In the 1980s and 90s, Zebra was pretty much known as the red-headed stepchild of mass market horror publishers. I'm glad to see that Zebra and their authors are getting more respect and interest these days, mostly due to Grady Hendrix's *Paperbacks From Hell.*

MMM: Behind *Hindsight* how many other manuscripts did you write?

KELLY: After *Hindsight,* I wrote seven more books for Zebra; *Pitfall, Something Out There, Moon of the Werewolf, Father's Little Helper, The Possession, Fear,* and *Blood Kin.* Two additional books were originally on their publishing schedule, *Hell Hollow* and *Restless Shadows,* but they shut down their horror line in 1996 and the manuscripts were returned to me. Those two were later published by Cemetery Dance and Thunderstorm Books.

MMM: Originally you *had* aspirations of becoming a comic book writer and artist in high school. You even did collaborations with classmate Lowell Cunningham who went off and created the *Men in Black* comic books. Do you still have those manuscripts today? What was Lowell Cunningham like in high school?

KELLY: Lowell and I became friends during our junior year. We both shared an interest in horror cinema and, of course, comic books. We began collaborating on several projects; Lowell doing the writing and me doing the artwork. I do still have a couple of the comics we did; *Ka, Son of Ra*—an Egyptian deity superhero—and *Wolf,* who was sort of a silver-haired covert operation ninja. Lowell was a great guy to work with—intelligent and reserved with a clever, dry wit about him. I remember after high school, he called me up and told me that he'd sold a series called *The Men in Black* to Malibu Comics. I said something like "Hey, that's great!" and sort of forgot about it after that. I was completely floored when I saw the first *Men in Black* movie years later and saw Lowell's name on the credits!

MMM:Your novels *Something Out There, Moon of the Werewolf, Blood Kin, The Buzzard Zone, Pitfall,* and *Fear* all feature monsters, bizarre beasts and creepy creatures. Do you think watching *Creature Feature* as a kid led to writing these books?

KELLY: I definitely think my childhood love for monster movies influenced me later on when I began writing. When I was in grade school, there was a local program that came on after school called *The Big Show*. They showed every old Universal monster and 50's era giant creature/science fiction movie you could imagine. Later on, when I was eleven or twelve, there was the Saturday night *Creature Feature* with host Sir Cecil Creepe. And, of course, I also built all the Aurora monster models and had my own movie projector. So, I was entirely immersed in the big monster craze of the 60s and early 70s. It's a love that's still there . . . one that probably will never go away.

MMM: How do you get out of a slump? With writing and sales?

KELLY: If I'm writing a story or a book and I feel like I'm spinning my wheels or beginning to lose interest in the progression of the storyline, I usually set it aside for a few days and work on something else . . . something entirely different in theme. If I feel particularly burnt out, I'll take a few days off and simply read. Reading, be it horror fiction or otherwise, tends to fire me up and grease up the gears again. Believe it or not, I simply don't worry about sales. After a book is published and I do my part promoting it, I focus on the next project. If you dwell too much on sales, reviews, and critical success, it can distract you and drag you down.

MMM: Of all the horror books you've written so far, which one was the easiest to write? And which one was the hardest? And why?

KELLY: The easiest one, without question, was *Fear*. I couldn't even tell you where the idea came from. I just woke up one morning with an inkling of an idea and started writing. The plot, the characters, the narrative . . . they all flowed so effortlessly. And putting as many nightmarish episodes as I could imagine into the storyline was incredibly fun. Just a wonderful writing experience all around.

The most difficult was probably *The Buzzard Zone*. It took me three years, on and off, to finish the book, and it wasn't even half as long as my old Zebra books. I think part of the problem was that it was a zombie book and, halfway through the writing, the zombie craze sort of fizzled out. Also, I knew I needed to come up with a fresh twist on the zombie legend, which I believe I pulled off successfully. I still think it's one of the best books I've written . . . it just didn't evolve as easily as the others.

MMM: How important is it for a new writer to get an agent these days?

KELLY: I would say it's very important if you're shooting for the major publishers. If you really want to get your work into the hands of an editor at one of the major NYC publishing houses, doing it through an agent is really the only way to go. However, if you're focusing on independent presses, like many horror writers are these days, then an agent probably wouldn't do you much good. In general, indie publishers are more respectful of those they publish and pay more reliably, or that's been my experience. Currently, I don't have an agent and, at this point in my career, I tend to take care of the business of submitting and promoting my work, and negotiating contracts myself.

MMM: How do you maintain an active fascination for horror?

KELLY: I've been in this business so long—going on 35 years—that sometimes it's difficult. I read a lot of work by new authors, because usually their perspective and vision is refreshing and more attuned to the times than mine is. That often excites me about the genre and gets my own creativity flowing again. I'll watch horror movies if they're good and suspenseful. I enjoy atmospheric horror more than bloody slasher storylines that have been overdone time and time again. Sometimes, I'll just harken back to my childhood days and indulge in some much-needed nostalgia. Dig out the old horror comics like *House of Mystery* or *Werewolf By Night*, or vintage copies of *Famous Monsters of Filmland*. Or I'll buy an old monster model I never had the pleasure of building and work on that. It sort of revives the little-boy monster lover that still lives inside me.

MMM: What advice would you give a new writer in horror?

KELLY: First, if you feel like you have the desire to write, do it. Don't procrastinate because you never went to college or never had writing lessons or you simply don't feel like you're good enough. There's a thousand reasons for not sitting down at a keyboard and beginning. If you have an idea for a story or novel in your head, it's up to you to bring it to fruition because it's all yours and nobody else is going to do it for you. Secondly, find your own voice. Don't strive to be the next Stephen King, strive to be a unique author with your own strengths and appeal. Also, diversify your fiction. Write about a different subject every time. When I worked for Zebra, I wrote about a different creature or situation with every new novel, not seven evil child or evil doll stories in a row like some authors.

MMM: If you could be a monster, which monster would you be and why?

KELLY: I suppose I would be the *Creature from the Black Lagoon.* At the age of six, that was the first monster movie I ever watched, and I've always had a soft spot for the Gill-Man. There's sort of a righteous justification for what he does. He's been isolated in his idyllic lagoon paradise on the Amazon for unknown years and suddenly invaders show up and violate his sanctuary. They have only one purpose in being there; to capture him and study him like a laboratory rat. Plus, they bring along a gorgeous brunette to tantalize him, when he's probably never enjoyed the company of a mate. One of the divers even shoots him with a harpoon. No wonder he wants to claw up everyone on the boat and rip their faces off. It's even worse in the second film, when they haul him all the way to Florida and imprison him in a tank, then resort to shock therapy to tame him.

MMM: Halloween is also featured in several of your books: *The Halloween Store & Other Tales of All Hallow's Eve, Mister Glow Bones & Other Halloween Tales,* and *Season's Greetings: Tales of Holiday Horror.* Is Halloween one of your favorite holidays and why?

KELLY: I have a great nostalgic love for Halloween. When I was a kid it was an all-month event. Me, my brother, and our friends planned it meticulously; the decorations, the costumes, the Trick-or-Treat route . . . everything was of great importance and had to be followed and completed down to the last detail. Plus, back then, kids had more freedom than they do now. Our parents would stay home to distribute candy and we'd roam all over town in the pitch dark, taking shortcuts through vacant lots and down shadowy alleyways . . . something you wouldn't dare let your kids do these days. I guess that's why I love to write about All Hallows' Eve so much. Horror fiction and Halloween naturally go hand in hand.

MMM: What was your inspiration for the book *Fear*?

KELLY: Like I said, the idea pretty much came out of the blue. But once I began writing and charting out the book, chapter by chapter, I decided to set it in post-World War II Tennessee in the rural town of Pikesville. I drew on experiences I had as a boy, plus developed characters based on people I'd known over the years. Then when it came to crossing over into Fear County, I had fun concocting every nightmarish episode imaginable. *Fear* has actually had a fresh resurgence of interest lately. The book is 27 years old, but many readers, both old and new, still love it. Many place it in their top ten favorite books of all time.

MMM: Last words?

KELLY: I just want to thank my old fans for sticking with me all these years, especially not giving up on me during my ten year hiatus away from the genre. Also, all the new readers who have discovered my work recently and enjoy it. As long as folks enjoy my brand of Southern-Fried horror, I'll certainly continue writing it.

"I was surprised Bubba (Ho-Tep) *was chosen, as it struck me as being difficult to film. But I was pleased with the results. I couldn't have fared better for my first time out. Well, unless it were a big hit."*

—Joe Lansdale

TERROR IS OUR BUSINESS
JOE LANSDALE

IT IS SURPRISING that Joe Lansdale's trophy shelf hasn't toppled over with all the honors bestowed on him over the years including ten Bram Stoker awards, the British Fantasy Award, American Horror Awards, Edgar, etc., etc., etc.

Lansdale has written in a number of genres: Horror, Western, Science Fiction, Mystery, and Suspense. A self-proclaimed writer of "Gumbo Fiction," and his writing is as spicy as a pot of Texas chili cooked all day on the range.

The Texan author has been writing for over three decades and has over 45 novels, in addition to several story collections, anthologies, and novellas to his credit, including *Fender Lizards, Dead in the West, Bubba and the Cosmic Bloodsucker, Freezer Burn, The Drive-In, The Magic Wagon, The Farside of the Cadillac Desert with Dead Folks, The God of the Razor, Dead on Bones: Pulp on Fire, Fishing for Dinosaurs and Other Stories, Miracles Ain't What They Used to Be,* which is a book of essays and memoirs, and many more.

He has been a student of the martial arts for more than thirty years. He's a two-time inductee into the International Martial Arts Hall of Fame, one such honor bestowed upon him for his founding of Shen Chuan, Martial Science. He's got the most decorated mantle in all of Nacogdoches.

Joe Lansdale lives in Nacogdoches, Texas, with his wife Karen, who is a writer and editor.

MORE MODERN MYTHMAKERS: Is there much of a difference between Northern and Southern writers?

JOE R. LANSDALE: I think there is, though perhaps not as great a difference as there once was. The South seems preoccupied with off-the-wall characters, a kind of gothic atmosphere. I think it makes Southern writing interesting.

Texas writing is similar to Southern writing, but it has a flavor all its own. Several. It's a big state and all the parts are different. Where I live is more Southern.

Texas is so wrapped up in myth and legend, it's hard to know what the state and its people are really about. Real Texans, raised on these myths and legends, sometimes become legends themselves. The bottom line is Texas, and its people are pretty much what most people mean when they use the broader term "America." No state better represents the independent spirit, the can-do attitude of America, better than Texas.

MMM: Were you surprised that Don Coscarelli the director and writer of the *Phantasm* movies turned your novella *Bubba Ho-Tep* into a movie. What are your thoughts on the motion picture?

LANSDALE: I was surprised *Bubba* was chosen, as it struck me as being difficult to film. But I was pleased with the results. I couldn't have fared better for my first time out. Well, unless it were a big hit. This one is going to be seen again and again and be a cult and collector's film. I'm proud of it.

MMM: We've already talked about *Bubba Ho-Tep*. But you also had several of your other works adapted for movies or television including *Incident On & Off the Road*, *Christmas with the Dead*, *Cold in July* and *Hap & Leonard* (TV series). What other of your works would you like to see on the big screen or television?

LANSDALE: A number of them would be nice. *Love, Death and Robots* did two short stories of mine the first season, one in the second. I loved writing for *Batman: The Animated Series*, and I'd love to do more in that vein. S*on of Batman* was a fun movie to like, but I'd like a crack at something darker in the DC Universe. *Batman* maybe, but without Robin. More Detective Comic style.

MMM: Besides the horror and crime novels, you have written some *Batman* material, including "Terror on The High Skies" and "Captured by The Engine" for the animated Batman series, and a couple of *Batman* short stories. Were you attracted to the character because he's a dark superhero? How much freedom do you have with a media character? Is there still a lot of creativity? What are some of your other comic book endeavors?

LANSDALE: I grew up on Batman, and actually, in the fifties, he was a two-fisted, honest, try-not-to-kill-the-bad-guy hero. But there was always some sort of implied darkness there, especially in Detective Comics. I like a hero who is at heart a Boy Scout but has had to adjust that thinking to the real world.

My favorite Batman work I've done is the "Batman" animated series, "Read My Lips," "Showdown," and maybe my all-time favorite, "Perchance to Dream."

"Critters" was fun, but the series had changed by then; dumbed down a bit and designed to appeal primarily to kids, where before it did that and appealed to adults as well.

I loved doing "Captured by The Engines" because I played Batman as real as possible, within the context of a superhero universe, and even a bit of writing experimentation. Of the two short stories, "Subway Jack" is my favorite because it's a perfect pulp piece with a kind of literary sensibility, and I got to use experimental approaches, comic frames, film, audio, the whole nine yards.

"Terror on the High Skies" was done for young kids, so I used the Batman of the fifties for that, the one I grew up on, with the weird gadgets, strange villain plans (a pirate ship that floats in the air), etc. It was a lot of fun and struck me as an episode of the comic from that era, though through the eyes of a kid.

MMM: The Bram Stoker Award is one of the highest honors a horror writer can get. You have won this award ten times, and a Lifetime Achievement. What does winning the Bram Stoker mean to you?

LANSDALE: Well, ten Bram Stokers, and another little house for Lifetime, I think. It's a great way to know the people in your field appreciate you. I don't think it changes your life, but it does make you feel good. Appreciate it, pleasure it, but don't think it means everything.

MMM: You've won several other awards as well: the British Fantasy Award, the Edgar Award, Raymond Chandler Lifetime Achievement Award. What awards are you the proudest of and why?

LANSDALE: I got a Golden Lion Award for continuing the legacy of Edgar Rice Burroughs. Probably that, out of nostalgia and feeling like I came full circle. Burroughs wasn't why I wanted to be a writer, but he was why I had to be.

MMM: Of all the books you've written, which one was the easiest to write and which one the most difficult to write?

LANSDALE: Several were fun to write. Few are truly easy, but some are easier than others. *The Bottoms*, *Mucho Mojo*, *Cold in July*, *Edge of Dark Water*, *Thicket*, all the Hap and Leonard novels came quickly. There have only been a few where I've struggled. It can be hard, and it can be hard work, but it's rarely hard work, though there is an exception now and then.

MMM: You have been writing since the '80s. What is the secret of your longevity, and how did you survive the '90s, when the suits said horror was dead?

LANSDALE: Horror may well have been dead. I started out writing crime and moved into horror, as I liked them both, but by the '90s I wasn't writing much in the way of horror. I was accepted as a crime writer, but it wasn't entirely planned.

I just went back to doing what I started out to do and the timing was good. I think I've survived by moving around and doing what I like, which goes against standard advice.

MMM: How many publishers saw *The Magic Wagon* before it was published by Doubleday?

LANSDALE: Only one, Doubleday. I sold it verbally to Pat LoBrutto, who then asked for a general outline, maybe a chapter or two, I don't remember. But only one publisher saw that one.

MMM: You have written *The Drive-In* and *The Drive-In 2*. If you had a real drive-in theater, what movies would you show?

LANSDALE: Oh, the movies in the book, and plenty of others. I'm not as nuts about the old bad ones as I once was. But there are certainly the usual suspects that are actually good films—*Phantasm*, *Texas Chainsaw Massacre*, *Night of The Living Dead* and *Bubba Ho-Tep*—and it has to do with them being great and having a wonderful atmosphere, not because I think they're low-budget films. They each are special in their own way.

MMM: How do you maintain an active fascination for horror?

LANSDALE: I actually read very little horror, and it's a smaller part of what I write. But I find that I have periods where I return to it as a writer and a reader. Weird and off-center fiction, crime fiction, is more what I do on a regular basis, but when horror circles back, I'm glad to hitch a ride. I just don't want any one kind of story, one kind of fiction, to hold me hostage. I read a book in the field now and then, a short story a little more often, but it's not my only reading matter, and is probably not even my most common fiction to read.

MMM: If you could be a monster, which monster would you be and why?

LANSDALE: Werewolf. Nice suit.

MMM: Of your collective works, what are your favorite three short stories and novels?

LANSDALE: "Night They Missed the Horror Show,"

"Stepping Out, Summer 68," "Mr. Weedeater." Today. Tomorrow I may like others. Novels: *The Bottoms, Mucho Mojo, The Drive-In*, though tomorrow I may like others. I really like the collection *High Cotton*, and it's my best short stuff. Of novellas, *On the Far Side Of The Cadillac Desert With Dead Folks, Bubba Ho-Tep*, which I wasn't nuts about at the time of the writing, *The Big Blow*, both the novella and the short novel version.

MMM: What was the inspiration for *God of the Razor*?

LANSDALE: I no longer remember. Seemed to have just jumped out full-blown.

MMM: You are friends with Dean Koontz. I did an interview with Mr. Koontz in the first book *Modern Mythmakers*. Care to share an anecdote of the Master of Suspense?

LANSDALE: Dean once called me and described a bug that was in his kitchen, and he wanted me to identify it. He doesn't like bugs and wanted it dead. Which was done, I think by an exterminator. It's been a while, but that's how I remember it.

MMM: What is the best advice another writer has ever given you?

LANSDALE: Sit down and write. I have my own version of that, and it's write like everyone you know is dead. Don't worry about other people's opinions. You write better that way. When you're finished, then you can hope there are readers like you. But the best fiction comes from a personal place.

MMM: What is your advice for the beginning writer?

LANSDALE: Once upon a time you wrote a story and put it in an envelope with return postage, and sent it to the editor of the magazine where you wanted it to appear, and they either returned it or bought it. My favorite was when they'd send a check back directly. Those days are gone. It's harder and harder to sell without an agent. The exception to that is short stories. I love short stories, and though there may not be as many markets as there once were, there are quite a few, especially if you're willing to go to on-line markets as well.

Short stories help you build a reputation and that helps you get an agent. But remember this, an agent can't sell something you can't sell, they just have more time to mess with it than you do. Their job is to make money off of your work, and yours is to write and make money off your work. So, agents are a necessary thing these days; long cry from when I managed my own career and sold my own short stories. It wasn't a big living, more like a part time job that didn't pay very well, but it sure helped me hone my craft. Good short stories teach you how to engage the reader and write nice, interesting, tight chapters.

I find that so many writers are so worried about having an agent that they forget they need to have the craft and the material first. That's the way to start. Write. Publish short stories. An agent most likely won't handle those anyway, as there's no money in it for them. But when you've got enough sales, some credits, and then you want to write that novel, then the agent might be more interested in listening.

DO IT FIRST. Then worry about selling it.

MMM: Last words?

LANSDALE: None, except, thanks.

MMM: You are most welcome, Joe.

"Artistically, horror's doing fantastic. The field's strength is that it constantly changes with the times, and there are always new young turks out to overthrow the old establishment."

—Bentley Little

WALKING ALONE
BENTLEY LITTLE

BENTLEY LITTLE HAS been writing sophisticated horror novels that explore more serious ideas than merely to scare. Throughout his career, the former Arizonian, now California writer has raised frightening fiction to the next level, where events are spooky and smart at the same time.

This is evident in his thirty novels such as *The Summoning, The Disappearance, The Policy, The Walking, The Town, The Store, The Ignored, University, His Father's Son, The Haunted, The Influence,* and *Gloria.*

An episode of *Masters of Horror* was based on his short story "The Washingtonians" and was directed by Peter Medak (*The Changeling* and *Species II.*).

For over three decades, Bentley Little has been building diehard fans with his novels and short story collections including Douglas Clegg, Brian Keene, director and screenwriter Shane Black, and horror luminaries such as Stephen King and Dean Koontz and the late, great Richard Laymon (which he talked about in the first edition of

Modern Mythmakers: 35 Interviews with Horror and Science Fiction Writers and Filmmakers).

MORE MODERN MYTHMAKERS: You started out getting published with Signet, then had a book published by Pinnacle, then you returned to Signet. You were with Signet for several years then you went to Cemetery Dance. Can you give more detail into the switching of publishers and why?

BENTLEY LITTLE: Actually, I was initially with St. Martin's Press, which published my first novel, *The Revelation*, in hardcover. I then went to New American Library, which put out *The Mailman* as a Signet paperback. Sales were so poor that NAL bribed me to use a pseudonym on my next novel, telling me that the book would be heavily promoted. It was not and *Death Instinct* came out with an Onyx paperback, I believe, and immediately tanked. There was no way in hell I was going to stay with NAL after that, so for my next novel *The Summoning*, I went to Zebra. The then-President of NAL, read *The Summoning,* liked it and asked why I wasn't with the company. They fired my old editor, lured me back with big bucks, and my books came out as Signet paperbacks for many years. Towards the end, however, things were not going well. NAL did not want me to write supernatural fiction, and for the first time, I had to have my ideas approved—which was how *His Father's Son* and *The Disappearance* came about (between editors, I snuck in *The Haunt* which was *not* officially approved). The writing was on the wall, though, and when NAL told me that my next novel would be released as an ebook, I bailed. Cemetery Dance offered to publish my work in both hardcover and paperback, and that's where I remain today.

MMM: Would you consider *The Influence, The Consultant,* and *The Bank* "economic horrors?" Do you feel the fear of losing money is universal?

LITTLE: *The Influence* definitely could be considered "economic horror," and I did conceive of the idea during the recession, but I would classify *The Bank* as more "institutional horror," along the lines of *The Mailman*, *The Policy*, or *The Association*. Although it does address economic issues, the novel is more concerned with set, structural elements of society that affect almost all aspects of modern life. *The Consultant* is a little different, and I'm not sure how I would classify it. Basically, it came about because I used to have a job where lily-livered management used consultants to validate or support decisions they had already decided to make, wasting huge amounts of money in the process. That always galled me, and I decided to write about it.

MMM: Your short story "The Washingtonians" (which was also published in *Fantastic Tales of Terror*) was on Showtime's *Masters of Horror* (directed by Peter Medak who also did *The Changeling* and *Species II*). How did it feel watching something you wrote being broadcast on television?

LITTLE: I was excited when I started watching it. I was horrified and humiliated by the time it was over. I loved *The Changeling* and was thrilled when I found out that Peter Medak would be directing the episode, but I thought he did a terrible job. Granted, the story does incorporate dark humor, but it's subtle. The episode was much broader, and I found the cartoonish tone just flat-out embarrassing. And the ending was godawful.

MMM: *The Store* has attracted some Hollywood attention too. Has there been any progress you can report?

LITTLE: *The Store* is the novel of mine that has most often been optioned for film. I think because its themes seem to be timely. It's currently under option for the fourth and fifth time, although nothing has yet come to fruition.

MMM: I've done a few interviews with you over the years. But we really haven't talked much about your writing process. Do you work from an outline or not? What are some of the ways you develop your characters? Rewriting?

LITTLE: My process is to just sit down and write. I generally have a basic idea of the plot, and who the main characters are, but peripheral characters I create as needed. I'm an instinctive writer, and nothing pre-thought-out. Things can (and usually do) change as I'm writing, depending on what I'm feeling or thinking, or in which direction the story seems to be going. It's a spontaneous process, which is why I would never use an outline. That would rain all the joy out of it for me. I need the freedom to improvise and add ideas as they occur.

MMM: Of your collected work, which was the easiest book to write, and which was the most difficult to write, and why?

LITTLE: *The Mailman* was probably the easiest for me to write because the story came to me fully formed, and I based the family on my family, and the town on our town. The hardest to write was probably *The Disappearance* or *His Father's Son* because I had no real connection to those stories. They were contractual fulfillment novels and writing them was a chore.

MMM: How do you get out of a slump? Writing and sales?

LITTLE: I never really had a writing slump, and sales slumps are out of my control, so I don't think about it.

MMM: You seem to be one of the few writers not using the internet. Why?

LITTLE: I think the internet is a great marketing tool, but marketing is not my job. My job is to write novels. It's my publisher's job to market and sell them. Also, like most writers, I'm a tremendous egoist, and If I did have internet access, I would probably waste far too much time defending myself against detractors and writing fake reviews touting how great my books are. I know this about myself, so I choose to avoid the temptation.

MMM: You don't make any public appearances such as at cons nor do book signings. You don't really do that many interviews. And you admit you don't network. Is this something that could impact the sales of your books?

LITTLE: Possibly. But I'm not going to be a dancing monkey just to get people to buy my books. My work is out there, and all my novels are still in print. Buy them or not. All I can do is write what I write and hope readers are interested. I should also point out that while I don't like going to conventions, I'm always happy to do interviews. It's just that nobody asks me.

MMM: Of all your novels you have written. Which one is your favorite?

LITTLE: *The Mailman* is my favorite. The family that's in the novel is based on my own family: me, my brother, and my parents. The town is our town. So I feel closer to this novel than any of the others.

I actually came up with the idea a couple of years before I wrote it. At that time, I was writing short stories for magazines that paid contributor copies. Every day I would go to the mailbox just to see if I got a rejection or acceptance letter; waiting for some kind of response for my submissions. I realized then how dependent writers are on the mail, how important were those five minutes of the day when the mailman came around. It's an admittedly skewed perspective, but I also realized that the mailman is the one individual who has daily contact with every person and every home. I extrapolated from there.

MMM: A strong predominant theme of yours is religion. Why do you think horror and religion work so well together?

LITTLE: Because they both deal with the big issues: life and death, good and evil. They also originate from a similar starting point, the Idea that the physical world is not all there is, that there are powers and entities beyond those of the material universe. Vampires, in particular, have always had a strong connection to religion, not only because, in western tradition, it is the accouterments of Christianity that are used to stop the monster, but also because the appeal of vampires is essentially the same as that of religion: a guarantee of immortality, the possibility of living forever. For the record, I am not all that religious myself.

MMM: Why did you use a lot of Biblical quotes in *The Revelation*?

LITTLE: *The Revelation* was my Master's project. But it wasn't a sensitive coming-of-age story or a chamber piece ruminating on a relationship. It was a flat-out horror novel. Which meant that I needed to have some sort of pretentious literary allusions in order to get it approved by the master's committee and thus earn my degree. I did this by pulling passages from The Bible and building the novel around those quotes so they would be seamlessly integrated into the story. I accomplished both my goals: I earned my master's degree *and* I wrote a horror novel.

MMM: How long did It take to get *The Revelation* published?

LITTLE: I wrote the book in 1986 and assumed that it would immediately be published, and I would become a rich and famous writer. Didn't happen. After sending the manuscript to publishers and receiving form rejection letters, I was forced to get a real job. I was living with my parents at the time, and my mom told me that Dean Koontz was going to be having a book signing at a nearby store for a limited edition of *Twilight Eyes*. She suggested I ask him for advice. I wasn't forward enough to do that, although I did go to the signing. I couldn't afford to buy *Twilight Eyes*, but I did bring along a bunch of my old paperbacks for him to sign. As luck would have it, we'd both had short stories published in the same magazine and got to talking. He asked if I'd written anything longer. I admitted that I had a novel I was trying to sell, and he took down my phone number. A few days later, he called and gave me the name of an agent, even dictating what I should say in my introductory letter. The agent, Dominick Abel, took me on as a client. Still, it took over a year for him to sell the novel, and it was a year after that the book finally came out—three years after I'd written it.

MMM: Is it flattering that some of horror's biggest names, like Stephen King and Dean Koontz, are fans of your writing?

LITTLE: It definitely is. I grew up reading both of them, so it's somewhat surreal that they now read my work. They have also been very generous with their support, and I doubt that I would be where I am today without them.

MMM: What are your thoughts about the horror field?

LITTLE: I live in my own little bubble, so I have no idea how well horror is doing commercially. But artistically, horror's doing fantastic. The field's strength is that it constantly changes with the times, and there are always new young turks out to overthrow the old establishment. That's the way it should be. It keeps the genre fresh.

MMM: Your mom attended the world premiere of *Psycho* a month before you were born. Is she a horror fan too?

LITTLE: Yeah. She was reading *The Exorcist* when I was in Junior High School. I was told I couldn't read the book because it had too much sex and violence. After she read it, the book was put in this box in the garage. I went out in the garage and read it. It's a family trait.

MMM: You've done two major short story collections, The *Collection* and *Walking Alone*? Do you see a third one in the future? Why or why not?

LITTLE: I continue to write short stories, so I'm sure there will be one sometime in the future, but collections do not sell as well as novels. Since writing is the way I make my living, I can't afford to put one out too often.

MMM: What's the hardest part of being a professional writer?

LITTLE: The uncertainty. Publishers' loyalties are not to authors but to sales figures. One poor selling book, and you might be out on your ear. I've managed to make a living writing fiction for over three decades now. But I'm one of the lucky ones. A lot of authors have fallen by the wayside. There were a lot of terrific writers in the 1980s and 1990s who seem to have completely disappeared. I don't know what happened to them, but I think about them sometimes and feel sad, because as a reader and fan, I've been deprived of their voices and stories they could have told. It's a dog-eat-dog business.

I write what I want to write. Period. I don't write novels-for-hire using media tie-in characters, I don't write suspense novels or thrillers. I write horror. And if no one wants to buy my books, I'll keep writing them until they do sell—and get a job at Taco Bell in the meantime. I won't compromise my fiction for the sake of remaining a "professional writer."

MMM: Last question, what advice would you offer for beginning writers?

LITTLE: Stay true to yourself. People always say "write what you know." But I think it's more important to write what you love. A good writer is a good writer no matter what genre.

"In broad strokes, The Reckoning *declares that wars have a life of their own, even after we've forgotten about them. War is a ghost that comes back to haunt us long after we thought it was buried."*

—Jeff Long

THE DESCENT
JEFF LONG

BY MICHAEL MCCARTY & CRISTOPHER DEROSE

JEFF LONG'S PASSION for climbing rigid mountains and traveling to exotic locales has been entertaining readers for years with his gripping novels. While he has also written the nonfiction books *Outlaw: The True Story of Claude Dallas, Duel of Eagles: The Mexican and US Fight for the Alamo,* and *Covering the Worlds of Edgar Rice Burroughs* (with Chris Wright).

The New York Times bestselling author is no stranger to the dark side of speculative literature, having penned such thrillers as *The Ascent,* which was inspired by his 1977 stint in a Nepalese prison, in a cell shared with the legendary wild men of the Mustang region above Annapurna. He would go on to take a cue from the genres of not only mystery and thriller, but also that of a thought-provoking ghost story for *The Reckoning.* He has also explored the complexities of primal horror in *The Wall,* dipped into an exploration of hell itself in *The Descent,* and has a short story collection called *Too Close to God.*

A self-described 'Oil rig brat,' Jeff spent his early years traveling from state to state, eventually landing in Colorado, where he learned how to shoot, fashion belts from rattlesnake hide, and was witness to nighttime apparitions, something that would seem to help him in his writing.

A novelist, nonfiction writer, historian, journalist, screenwriter, and natural risk-taker, Jeff isn't one to shy away from the physical risks either. He climbed such mountains as Everest, the Himalayas, and Makalu. His other adventures landed him in jail on smuggling charges, or the unique risks inherent in traveling to Cambodia and Bosnia where he served as an election supervisor for those countries' first democratic elections.

His books have won several awards including the Texas Literary Award, the Western Writers of America Spur Award for Best Novel, The British Boardman-Tasker Award for Mountain Literature, the Banff Mountain Book Fiction Grand Prize, and the American Alpine's Club Literary Award.

As much as an adventurer he is in real life, it doesn't compare to the adventures of the mind that his books have taken readers on for over two decades, beginning with his debut novel, *Angels of Light,* in 1987.

MORE MODERN MYTHMAKERS: Which came first: your love of suspense/horror, or climbing?

JEFF LONG: Nineteen sixty-three was my banner year for both; that was the year Americans first reached the summit of Mt. Everest, which totally enthralled me. I was in seventh grade. Around the same time, I bought my first book, a paperback edition of *Dracula.* The Everest event infected me for life. The *Dracula* event forced me to sleep with a wooden crucifix on my chest until halfway through eighth grade. The two converged years later when I was soloing a wall called the Diamond. Halfway up, I spent the night in a hammock. Midnight came, and with it a vampire, his nails scratching on the rock. I even felt him/her clawing at my hammock, and knew for a fact I wouldn't make it until dawn. But I made it (at least I think I did), and by the light of day, I figured out that my night visitor had been mice that live in the cracks up there.

MMM: Since you wrote a book with the same title, what did you think of the movie *The Descent?*

LONG: I'm still astonished by the identical elements, story setup, title, and monsters. Isn't one advised to be flattered in such circumstances? Or hire a lawyer? All I can imagine is that the director/writer, who keeps howling that there are no similarities, must have drunk too much warm English beer.

MMM: Why did you decide to write about hell in *The Descent*?

LONG: Back in my all-boy, Catholic high school, I was introduced to Dante's *Inferno* by Brother Bernard. He was a Golden Gloves champion who brooked no silliness, and freely powdered offenders with the chalkboard eraser thrown with amazing velocity and precision. I was desperately trying to stay awake—either during Brother Bernard's lecture about Dante's *Inferno,* or was it in a Franciscan monastery in northern New Mexico—when my eye fell upon a crack in the floor. One thing led to another, and suddenly I found myself constructing an expedition into the circles of hell. Years later, following the publication of my Everest novel (*The Ascent*), I was groping for a next topic to write about. I saw *The Ascent* on a bookshelf, upside down, and that instantly suggested *The Descent*. In the same instant, my hell expedition came swarming up in Technicolor.

MMM: Was Satan modeled after anyone in *The Descent?*

LONG: No. Other characters were, though. If Dante could consign his enemies to various circles of eternal suffering, then I decided, why shouldn't I do the same? I only hope my enemies recognize themselves getting skewered, roasted, and served up. By the way, I'm adding to Dante's circles a special spot in hell for plagiarists.

MMM: Were you influenced by Dante's *Inferno* in *The Descent*?

LONG: That and Jules Verne's *Journey to the Center of the Earth,* H.G. Wells' *The Time Machine* and *The Circular Labyrinth*, by Jorge Luis Borges. Hell's a wonderful place to visit.

MMM: Who is more monstrous in *The Descent,* the humans or the monsters?

LONG: That's the question I'm asking throughout my *Descent* trilogy. Most of your stock Hollywood monsters are just animals with an appetite for humans. They're grizzly bears or man-eating lions dressed up as aliens or predators. But a bear isn't evil, it's just doing what bears do, though I have to say, one of the greatest horror movies in recent time was Herzog's *Grizzly Man*. My mission in the trilogy is to probe for deep horror and true monstrosity. In my hunt for the devil, I'm asking if pure evil exists.

In the first book of the trilogy, *The Descent*, my answer to the question of pure evil is no, that pure evil is relative and a shared responsibility. I kill off the leader of the subterranean hominids, the historical Satan who rules hell's monsters. At least he's the character we presume to be Satan, and that seems to be the end of it. *The Descent* is basically a Western horror—Western, as in our conquest of the frontier. Just as we came to admit the humanity of the *red devils* over time, *The Descent* exposes recognizable bits and pieces of the monsters' sameness with us, or our sameness with them.

But in my second and third books of the *Descent* trilogy, I'm exploring monstrosity at a whole other level. The monsters of *The Descent* have been largely exterminated, and a different kind of monster emerges. A real fallen angel exists. If there is such a thing as pure evil, it must reside in him, so the myths go. In Deeper, the second book, the angel is holed up in a subterranean chamber, something like bin Laden in his mountain cave. Now I get to have a dialogue with the ultimate villain. I mean to find out what makes him tick, and whether or not monsters can be more monstrous than we are.

MMM: What can you tell us about your sequel to *The Descent* called *Deeper*?

LONG: *Deeper* is the second book in the *Descent* trilogy. The third book will be called *Deliverance*, with a monumental tip of the hat to James Dickey. It picks up the story, landscape and two characters about ten years after *The Descent*. In the first book, we go down to find "them." In the second book, "they" come up after we wrote them off as an extinct species. The "fallen" angel—call him Satan, Santa, or Joe—makes his real debut in *Deeper*. Human virtues and vices get another workout in the search for missing children. At the center is a question I pondered in *The Descent* and will continue to ponder through *Deliverance,* and that is, "What is the face of God?"

MMM: *The Reckoning* can be seen as having a rather ambiguous narrative. It may or may not have a happy ending, for instance. Is there a definitive ending?

LONG: Yes. In broad strokes, *The Reckoning* declares that wars have a life of their own, even after we've forgotten about them. War is a ghost that comes back to haunt us long after we thought it was buried.

MMM: *The Reckoning* was also a search book, a search for an American pilot in Cambodia. Did you get any feedback from Vietnam veterans about the book?

LONG: I consulted a colonel with the military unit that went into Cambodia during the Vietnam War, and fictionalized that unit and events. I also consulted with JPAC, the official military "archangel" which continues to search for the missing soldiers of past American wars. Several close friends were Vietnam vets, and helped me with details.

MMM: What was the inspiration for *The Reckoning?*

LONG: Back in 1992, I visited a friend with the U.N. in Cambodia. The Khmer Rouge were still active in the west, but we decided to chance a visit to Angkor Wat. Not too surprisingly, the place was empty, not a Westerner anywhere. Gunfire crackled in the far distance. There were a few monks and forest children, plus these solitary, sticklike survivors of the camps who wandered through the ruins like ghosts. It was a powerful stage for a ghost story. But I felt the story needed characters that American readers could relate to, and that defied me for another few years. Then I heard about a forensic unit with the U.S. military. Their mission is to find the remains of missing soldiers from past wars, particularly the Vietnam War, and that included digs in Cambodia. What if, I wondered, my ghosts were searching for their own remains? What if they had no idea they were ghosts? The story took off from there.

MMM: The Vietnam War is long over, but in *The Reckoning* the horrors persist. Why?

LONG: History is the biggest haunted house of them all. The Vietnam War helped shape my whole generation, and our children's, too, even if the children have no memory of it. But wars have a way of unleashing strange ghosts and demons long after the fact. They call to us. They demand our memory of them. Think about the power of the Missing In Action lobby, back before 9/11. It wasn't just the MIA families that were haunted. To one degree or another, we were all captive to impossible hopes and memories. It was true with Vietnam and, in a few years, it will be true with Iraq and Afghanistan. We don't own our wars. Wars own us.

MMM: *Year Zero* is about the search for historical Jesus. Did your religious convictions strengthen or weaken when writing this novel?

LONG: According to some evangelicals who took the time to correspond with me, I have no religious convictions. In fact, I took on the historical Jesus after setting out to find the historical Satan (in *The Descent*.) Both are wildly fertile characters, especially if you try to set them in a real life context. Long ago, while writing a history of the Alamo battle (*Duel of Eagles*,) I learned that nothing makes a character more poignant than his or her warts and clay feet. When you can connect to a protagonist—god or not (and in Texas, Davy Crockett is a god)—at a gritty, personal level, then you rise above a reader's natural voyeurism and begin to feel and taste their suffering, sacrifices, and joys. That's the writer's biggest challenge, making a character really come alive.

MMM: How do you define "Fiction in High Definition?"

LONG: I sometimes wonder how many other writers actually listen to their readers. Certainly I do. This isn't the first time I've been asked what the hell "Fiction in High Definition" means, and had to fake an answer. To be honest, I can't remember what the hell "Fiction in High Definition" meant in the first place. So I've changed it on my website to "Extreme Fiction," because I usually write about the edge of the abyss.

MMM: Climbers can be a superstitious bunch. What are some of yours?

LONG: Keep your flip-flops and shoe soles down on the floor, never tipped (I learned that one in Nepal.). Never step over someone's legs (Tibet). Never, ever touch the head of a monk (detonates your karma). Always try to have an extra pair of dry socks (expedition habit). If possible, walk clockwise around just about anything: chortens, cows lying in the road, sacred mountains). Don't ride shotgun in countries with landmine problems (the front and outside seat usually takes the brunt of any explosion.). Keep your knots tight (shoelaces, climbing harness, anchor knots). And the number thirteen is lucky (at least it works for me).

MMM: What made you write *Duel of Eagles*?

LONG: Two things: first, I was born in Texas, and wanted to connect some circles. And second, I was inspired by Evan Connell's *Son of the Morning Star* about Custer and the Last Stand. It was an incredibly fine history written with a novelist's palette, and furthermore written after whole bookshelves of other works on the man and the battle. When I first began researching, my goal was merely a better told version of the same old tale. But as I quickly discovered, there was an entirely different reality to the myth. (Davy) Crockett very probably surrendered and was executed. Travis took liquid mercury as a medicine for his syphilis, and was possibly insane. (James) Bowie was a brutal slave runner. Above all, the battle that has come to exemplify national defense (with its line in the sand,) was, in fact, part of an American invasion of Mexico that didn't end until we had taken two-fifths of Mexico as part of our Manifest Destiny.

MMM: Have any of your books creeped you out more than others?

LONG: I've tried to invest all of my recent books with the best demons and most creative horror I can. *The Descent* is full of the darkest savagery I could conjure. *Year Zero* was my take on the American Apocalypse. *The Wall* opens with a 3,000 foot-fall off of El Cap and tapped into my vampire-on-the-Diamond experience, plus the natural dread of climbing. *Deeper* plunges into the old abyss. Whatever I've feared, I try to confront it on the page.

MMM: If you could be any monster, which monster would you be and why?

LONG: The fallen angel. He's seen it all, including the face of God.

MASTERS: Last words?

LONG: Thanks for inviting me to MORE MODERN MYTHMAKERS.

MMM: You are most welcome, Jeff.

"George (Romero) and I had a lot of calls after that. Some were about the book, of course; and many were about books, TV, and movies in general. We ranged far beyond the topics of zombies. George had so much experience in pop culture that our conversations ran deep. He became a good friend."

—Jonathan Maberry

GHOST ROAD BLUES
JONATHAN MABERRY

BY HOLLY ZALDIVAR & MICHAEL MCCARTY

JONATHAN MABERRY IS a New York Times bestselling author, 5-time Bram Stoker Award-winner, 3-time Scribe Award winner, Inkpot Award winner, and comic book writer. His vampire apocalypse book series, *V-WARS*, was a Netflix original series. He writes in multiple genres including suspense, thriller, horror, science fiction, fantasy, and action, for adults, teens, and middle grades. His novels include the Joe Ledger thriller series, *Bewilderness*, *Ink*, *Glimpse*, the *Pine Deep* trilogy, the *Rot & Ruin* series, the *Dead of Night* series, *Mars One*, *Ghostwalkers: A Deadlands* novel, and many others.

He is the editor of many anthologies including *The X-Files, Aliens: Bug Hunt, Don't Turn Out the Lights, Nights of the Living Dead,* and others. His comics include *Black*

Panther: DoomWar, Captain America, Pandemica, Highway to Hell, The Punisher, and *Bad Blood*. He is a board member of the Horror Writers Association, president of the International Association of Media Tie-in Writers, and the editor of *Weird Tales* Magazine. Visit him online at www.jonathanmaberry.com

MORE MODERN MYTHMAKERS: The best and most effective horror tries to investigate what we think of ourselves and what it means to be us. Washington Irving's tales, for example, generally wrestle with the question of what it means to be an American in the post-Revolutionary War period. Nathanial Hawthorne battled with the intellectual promise of a nation rising to international credibility, while simultaneously choking under the yoke of a Puritan past. Stephen King made a name for himself chronicling the slow collapse of the American small-town way of life. What do you think the zombie and its current popularity is telling us about ourselves?

JONATHAN MABERRY: Zombies are not crisis-specific, in terms of how they are used as metaphors in popular entertainment. First, though, a note of clarification—the 'zombie' we think of when discussing the monster genre tends to be a wholly fictional flesh-eating ghoul of the kind first presented by George Romero in *Night of the Living Dead* (1968). They are not a cultural phenomenon from Haitian folklore or religious beliefs. The zombie label was hung on Romero and post-Romero monsters by Italian film distributors. That said, the zombies we make movies, TV shows, comics, novels, and games about tend to be a very elastic Big Bad for all kinds of stories. With no enduring specific legacy of the kind vampires, werewolves, and other more classically established creatures, the zombie is there to be used based on the needs of the writer.

Zombies—and the apocalyptic crash of our known and

comforting infrastructure—represent any kind of massive, shared threat. They are an easy threat to understand, and we are so comfortable with the inevitable destruction of all we know, from the reliability of first responders ever showing up to the paranoia of having loved ones become predatory monsters, that we quickly take it all as read. Then, once the crisis has been established, the zombie itself often fades into the background of the story, reappearing when we (a) need an action moment, (b) we need to remind ourselves of the severity of the crisis, (c) we need a reminder of the enormity of what has been lost, and (d) we need a big, splashy finale. This latter is often crafted to show either the heroism of the last survivors or the futility of it all—or both.

That said, this creates, for storytellers, a black canvas on which any kind of story can be painted. Max Brooks, in his novel *World War Z,* used the zombie apocalypse to take an unflinching look at the consequences of global politics, political game-playing, and human greed. And much of it was echoed in our recent Covid pandemic.

Isaac Marion's *Warm Bodies* explored how human contact can bring us back from the uber-hypnosis of addiction to the routine of day-to-day living. George Romero explored similar themes in *Diary of the Dead,* filmed during the early days of social media when people were so busy looking at devices they did not look around at the real world.

Brian Keene explored existentialism in *The Rising,* where a threat emerges that is so vast there is simply no chance for survival—a topic made popular by H.P. Lovecraft's cosmic horror tales. And David Wellington spun a similar tale with slightly more optimism (or, perhaps less deliberate cynicism) with his trilogy *Monster Island, Monster Nation*, and *Monster Planet.*

Mike Carey's innovative *The Girl with All the Gifts*, uses an alien-spore-based zombie apocalypse to explore issues of being different and marginalized (the little zombie girl who is hated for what she is to the point no one cares *who* she is), and other themes.

I used my novels *Dead of Night* and *Fall of Night* to explore the horror of diseases such as dementia and Alzheimer's, and how the people we love start leaving us while still alive, becoming essentially aliens to our memory of them; and whose progressive mental and physical decay offers daily proof of a living death. And my *Rot & Ruin* series of young adult post-apocalyptic zombie novels focus on the effects of a prolonged crisis on the adult population—creating a pervasive PTSD; and how the younger generation struggles for optimism about their own lives.

And so on. Every significant piece of zombie storytelling uses the monsters to unpack the emotional, social, political, personal, or cultural dynamics of their chosen topic. And the zombies, lacking actual personality, never interfere in what are, in truth, explorations of the human being in crisis.

MMM: You're certainly a master and no stranger to how you write your horror fiction. Would you mind explaining a bit about the other fiction you write? How do you approach these genres?

MABERRY: I read across genre lines and always have. It's no surprise that I choose to write in whatever genre appeals to me. Even when I sat down to write my first novel—*Ghost Road Blues,* lead-off to the Pine Deep Trilogy—I knew that once that series was done, my next book was likely to be in a different genre. I made sure to pick a literary agent who was able to hang with me as I shifted lanes. Sara Crowe, formerly of Trident Media, and now with Pippin Properties, has been a great partner (accomplice...?) in this. She not only supports my cross-genre writing but often encourages it.

My desire to do this sort of thing came directly from a conversation I had with Richard Matheson (*I Am Legend, Stir of Echoes, What Dreams May Come)* when I was 13.

He told me to avoid being pigeonholed in one genre because it would limit my creative growth and thereby keep doors closed that might otherwise lead to success and fulfillment.

My fourth novel was a weird-science thriller, *Patient Zero*, and the first of what has become my longest-running series. Each book is built around a different kind of threat (transgenics, drones, weaponized rabies, etc.).

I keep looking for new ways to have creative fun. I've done straight science fiction (*Mars One),* speculative sci-fi fantasy (*Bewilderness*), Weird West Steampunk alt-history (*Ghostwalkers: A Deadlands Novel)*, media tie-in (*The Wolfman, X-Files Origins: Devil's Advocate*), suspense (*Glimpse*), and, as of early 2022, epic fantasy (*Kagen the Damned*). In short fiction I've stretched even further, with stories in the genres of mystery, thriller, horror, comedy, historical fantasy, military science fiction, Old West, crime, and others; as well as plating in the worlds created by others as part of the genre of media tie-in fiction (*Wizard of Oz, True Blood/Sookie Stackhouse, C.H.U.D., Plan 9 from Outer Space, Aliens, Predator, John Carter of Mars, Hellboy,* and a slew of others.)

MMM: How do you maintain an active fascination for horror?

MABERRY: It's a scary world out there. In my first novels I wrote about what scared me or which scared me at different times in my life: child abuse, abandonment issues, intolerance, etc.). In later works I explored what scares other people. Much of this forms the basis of what I write in the horror genre. Horror fiction allows us to explore our fears in ways that can—because we are the god of our individual literary universe—allow us to contain the threat and take agency over what scares us. We give real life horrors a better third act. The monsters, like zombies, are stand-ins for our own fears.

My grandmother introduced me to all things scary. She was essentially an old lady version of the super-credulous Luna Lovegood from the Harry Potter novels. She believed in everything from ghosts to church grims. All of it. And she filled my young mind with tales of things that go bump in the night. She also encouraged me to read anthropology, psychology, archaeology, and scientific speculation in order to understand why some monsters were created. For example, SIDS (sudden infant death syndrome), is a likely cause of some vampire beliefs where an unholy spirit enters a house and sucks away the breath or life force of an otherwise healthy child. Believing that a monster did this, rather than accepting that a loving god would arbitrarily kill a child, provided a measure of comfort because the family members had action steps to follow—prayers, communion, holy objects used for protection. And since SIDS rarely strikes the same family twice, these 'cures' seemed to work, thereby reinforcing religious faith and adherence to the advice of the local priest.

Knowing the real-world answers behind beliefs balances perspective, and for a writer it opens all sorts of creative doors. It's really how I learned to use monsters as metaphors. This means that there is no end to the number of stories I can tell in the horror genre, even if that horror story is an element of a tale I'm telling in a completely different genre (thriller, mystery, science fiction, etc.).

MMM: What is it about ghosts that attracts your attention? Do you believe ghosts really exist?

MABERRY: I am not as credulous as my grandmother was, but I keep a very open mind. Rather than saying "I don't believe" in something that cannot, currently, be either proven or disproven; I prefer to say that I am very open to proof. I've never seen a ghost, but have read compelling articles, books, and stories. I know many people who do believe them, and because ghost beliefs are arguably the most common supernatural belief—and present in every human culture; it's an easy conversation to have with people. Readers will read a ghost story more quickly than, say, a gory zombie tale, or a terrifying werewolf novel. It's, to a degree, safer. After all, with all the ghost hunter shows, how often has there been an 'attack' by a spirit? I can't think of any, so it allows people to believe in the other world, to whatever degree suits them, without feeling as directly threatened by it.

MMM: In the wake of the post Covid-19 pandemic, have your thoughts on your books *Pandemica, Patient Zero, Lost Roads, Still of Night, Dead of Night* and others changed in any way?

MABERRY: Well, Covid directly impacted two of my higher-profile projects. My first TV series, *V-Wars*, on Netflix, launched just before the pandemic began. Because it was a grim story about an outbreak, viewing numbers that had been huge at the launch, tailed off dramatically once Covid was a household word. As a result, we did not get a second season pickup.

And I'd been writing a comic book, *Pandemica*, for IDW Publishing, which dealt with an outbreak of a weaponized virus that targeted ethnic groups. There were themes of white supremacy, political game playing and obfuscation, and more. That was written in 2019 but released as a series of single issues in early 2020. The similarities in my story, plus the shuttering of comic book stores, nearly killed the series. The final (of five) planned issues was delayed by months. The publisher released the whole series in trade paperback form that were sold online and in bookstores—not comics shops—before the fifth issue was finally released. But, again, people were a bit less sanguine about reading a plague story that so closely paralleled real life. Once the vaccines were out, the sales of that trade collection began to rise.

In novels I wrote during the pandemic, Covid was a theme that had to be addressed in order to allow the reader to more easily suspend disbelief. Its absence would have been noticeable and anomalous.

MMM: What authors do you have on your bookshelf that you re-read, and perhaps motivate you when you've hit a blank page, or to clear the fog of a difficult scene?

MABERRY: Oddly, I don't get writer's block and am not stymied by the blank page. I read a lot for entertainment and to study the craft of my colleagues. Authors whose works I return to include James Lee Burke, Christopher Golden, Shirley Jackson, HP Lovecraft, Edgar Allan Poe, Joe R. Lansdale, M.R. James, Graham Masterton, Robert McCammon, and Michael Moorcock.

To get me in gear for writing prose, I read poetry aloud every day and have for quite some time. The poets' ability to condense complex visual and emotional imagery into a few brief lines is enchanting. The best ones do that without forcing the reader into one specific interpretation, which is something the very best novelists can do as well. It's an invitation to co-create the story as it's being read. So, that is something I do daily. But when I read prose fiction, it's for the deep love of the stories told and the skills used to craft them.

MMM: What are some of your theories as to what you think begins the zombie apocalypse? What causes people to turn into zombies in the first place and why does this occur?

MABERRY: I've explored different possible causes for the zombie apocalypse, from weaponized prions to parasites. I have a handful of top scientists I use as my experts, and they take my wacky literary theories and help guide me toward rational explanations. Well, as rational as possible.

The most practical cause of the zombie apocalypse I've written about was the one presented in the *Dead of Night* series, which formed the backstory for the entire *Rot & Ruin* novels. It's an old Cold War bioweapon based on real parasites whose attack essentially rewires the target host and turns them into incubators for their young as well as defenders of those larvae. The green jewel wasp, toxoplasma, and others, used in conjunction. I worked that one out with the help of parasitologists, molecular biologists, and epidemiologists. We got the science to about 70% doable based on real-world science. Luckily that last 30% is not at all doable, and we can all be happy about that.

MMM: You were introduced to the horror genre rather young and through an interesting group of people. What were these unusual beginnings?

MABERRY: When I was in middle school, the librarian there was the secretary for two groups of professional writers, one that met in my hometown of Philadelphia, and one that met infrequently in New York. The Philly group, known as the Hyborian Legion, were devotees of sword and sorcery fiction, with a strong bias toward the Conan stories. One of the founding members was L. Sprague de Camp, who brought Conan back from obscurity and expanded upon the oeuvre.

The New York thing was really a series of parties hosted by a big exec in the publishing world. They met whenever there were enough notable genre writers in town. I would go up there with the librarian almost every month, and so got to meet this constantly changing menagerie of legendary writers. Over the three years we went to those events I met Ray Bradbury, Richard Matheson, Harlan Ellison, Avram Davidson, Arthur C. Clarke, Robert Bloch, and others. Of those, Bradbury and Matheson kind of took me under their wings. They would bring me shopping bags full of books—theirs and others. And, because the librarian told them that I was very serious about wanting to be a writer, they would offer a lot of advice, both on the craft of writing and the business of publishing. They also introduced me to the genres of horror, fantasy, and science fiction. Until then, I'd been reading a lot of Edgar Rice Burroughs, Ed McBain, and Robert E. Howard. They expanded on that. Their understanding of the history and legacies of horror fiction was profound, and it's because of them I was introduced to Shirley Jackson, Manly Wade Wellman, John W. Campbell, H.G. Wells, M.R. James, H.L. Mencken, Daphne du Maurier, Arthur Machen, Sheridan Le Fanu, Tom Tryon, Henry James, Elizabeth Gaskill, Robert W. Chambers, Lord Dunsany, Ann Radcliffe, Guy de Maupassant, and so many others.

MMM: The original *Weird Tales Magazine* was published from 1923 to 1954. What caused you to work on resurrecting the magazine?

MABERRY: I was first contacted to write a story for the rebirth of the magazine, and I did—an historical fantasy with elements of cosmic horror, "The Shadows Beneath the Stone." Shortly after turning it in, they asked if I was interested in editing the whole issue. Naturally, I jumped at the chance because I love *Weird Tales*. I was introduced to it—nearly simultaneously—by Ray Bradbury (who'd written for it) and L. Sprague de Camp (because of Conan).

I accepted the gig with the understanding that I would curate the issue. They agreed, and I reached out to some writers I know and trust to give me killer stories that showcased a variety of storytelling styles. That first issue (#363) included stories by Victor LaValle, Sherrilyn Kenyon, Josh Malerman, Lisa Morton, Hank Schwaeble, and poetry by Stephanie W. Wytovich. On the masthead I was listed as 'editorial director,' but the editor was older and ill, so I was allowed to work on it myself.

By the second issue, I was moved up to editor and remain so. The second issue included works by Seanan McGuire, Dacre Stoker & Leverett Butts, Joe Lansdale, Rena Mason, Tim Waggoner, Weston Ochse, Lee Murray, Linda Addison, Alessandro Manzetti, Gregory Frost, and newcomer Marguerite Reed. I just wrapped #365, which is the third of my 'unthemed' issues. Then I began building themed issues, and was lucky to nab an excerpt of Michael Moorcock's latest *Elric* novel; as well as original stories by Kevin J. Anderson, Tamora Pierce, and others. After that will be a cosmic horror issue, and then an occult detective issue.

It's incredibly gratifying, and an amazing honor, to edit such a legendary and influential magazine as *Weird Tales*. I am celebrating diversity within the pages by bringing in writers of all gender orientations, all races, and varied cultural backgrounds. There are a lot of ways to be weird and scary, and with a more inclusive structure we can present stories so outré to the average reader that we're able to surprise and (I hope) delight them.

MMM: What was the underlying motivation for *Glimpse*? What about *Ink*?

MABERRY: *Glimpse* and *Ink* are two of my favorite works I've ever done. Both are explorations of 'little horror,' meaning that they aren't much more personal and intimate explorations of fear, horror, and terror than I typically address in my apocalyptic fiction. *Glimpse* is about a young woman, newly clean after years of drug addiction, who is attempting to rebuild her life. She begins having glimpses of a little terrified boy, and she begins to realize these are contemporary visions of the child she gave up for adoption when she was 16. The villain of that piece, Doctor Nine, is a kind of vampire who feeds on the last drops of hope in the human soul.

Ink began as an exploration into the reasons people get tattooed—why they chose certain images, does the meaning change over time, etc. Though not inked myself, I am fascinated by that world. After conducting hundreds of interviews with people who have tattoos, I found that there was a notable percentage whose tattoos are tied to their most precious memories—loss, war, love, etc. So, being a horror writer, that sparked a story idea about someone – another non-typical vampire—who was able, through a simple touch, to steal the tattoos connected to precious memories, and then both live those memories in their fullness, and also feed on them. The person who lost the tattoo gradually loses the memory, which can be quite a horrible experience. One character loses all memories of her murdered child. I found the thought of that to be quite horrifying and had to dive deep into it and tell that story.

MMM: The first ten novels of the Joe Ledger series have him and his team working with the Department of Military Sciences, a clandestine organization that deals with cases Homeland Security can't handle. However, *Rage* and *Relentless* feature Joe leading the Rogue Team as part of an international agency. Why is Joe Ledger now working internationally?

MABERRY: There are several reasons why I shifted the Ledger series of a domestic counter-terrorism group to a bunch of international troubleshooters.

First, I love world history, politics, and cultural diversity. I wanted to feed my own love of researching new things by stretching beyond my comfort zone.

Second, the change happened midway through a presidency that I found to be dangerous, clueless, and absurd. I could not rationalize a group of elite shooters run by a brilliant a-political man like Mr. Church remaining under the thumb of such a president.

Third, it offers my characters greater freedom to pick their own cases.

And fourth, it creates a nice jumping on point for new readers who may be intimidated by so many previous novels.

MMM: How did you meet the late, great George Romero? What is your favorite memory of your friendship with him?

MABERRY: I was a fan of Romero's since I snuck into the movies at age 10 to see the world premiere of *Night of the Living Dead*. I first met him when we were both on a panel discussion at a genre convention. I manfully refrained from being too obvious a fanboy. Then we kept winding up on zombie panels here and there. It was clear we shared many of the same ethics and views on politics, racism, and other key topics. We began chatting before and after the panels and had coffee together. When I wrote *Dead of Night,* I dedicated it to George, and later learned that he considered it to be his favorite zombie novel.

Roll forward a few years and I had a conversation with my editor at St. Martin's Griffin and said that I had been thinking about editing a zombie anthology and wanted to see if we could get permission to have those stories set officially in the world of *Night of the Living Dead.* He said if I could get Romero's blessing then we had a deal. So, I called George and explained that I wanted to do the book, with all of the stories set in the 72 hours surrounding his landmark film. George said that he'd agree on three conditions. His first was that he wanted to co-edit it with me. That surprised and delighted me, and I agreed at once. The second condition was that he wanted to write a story for that book. Another resounding yes. The third condition completely floored me. He said that he loved *Dead of Night* and its sequel, *Fall of Night*, so much that he wanted me to write a story for the book that took his favorite character (Sam Imura, from *Fall*) and brought him from the end of that book to the farmhouse in his first zombie movie). That meant that he was telling me that he wanted my books to be official prequels to his movies, which made my Young Adult *Rot & Ruin* series to be official sequels. Naturally, I agreed and may have been rather tearful and emotional after the call (it's entirely possible). Talk about a dream come true.

George and I had a lot of calls after that. Some were about the book, of course; and many were about books, TV, and movies in general. We ranged far beyond the topics of zombies. George had so much experience in pop culture that our conversations ran deep. He became a good friend.

Our book, *Nights of the Living Dead*, debuted five days before his death, and it was the last project he completed before he passed. I hope it stands as a fitting tribute to a great man and one of the most influential creators of all time. After all, how many authors can you name who created an entire genre?

MMM: You spent twenty-five years writing nonfiction—articles, columns, even textbooks. What was it about fiction that caused you to seriously study the genre and ultimately write your first novel, *Ghost Road Blues*?

MABERRY: After writing so many books about martial arts and self-defense, I wanted to do one that would have pleased my grandmother. So, I wrote a hefty nonfiction book called *The Vampire Slayers Field Guide to the Undead,* written under a pen name (at my, then, publisher's insistence). Researching that book reignited my love of horror, particularly the folkloric versions of vampires, werewolves, etc. However, I was frustrated by not being able to find many novels that used those folkloric monster forms. Most were variations on the standard Hollywood versions, and those takes on blood drinkers and lycanthropes had no real corollary in folklore. For example, in folklore vampires do not need to be invited in, they are not afraid of sunlight (even Dracula walked around during the day), they were not killed by stakes (those were used to hold it down for decapitation, or to pin it into the coffin), and crosses had no effect on them. Much of what we "know" about those monsters are really literary devices created by writers. So, I decided to try my hand at writing a novel with folkloric versions of the monsters. Unlike the *Slayers Guide* I'd written as 'Shane MacDougall,' I wanted the fiction to be published under my own name.

I'd studied journalism in college and never taken a creative writing course. So, I had to teach myself how to write fiction. Luckily, I remembered a lot of the advice I'd gotten from Bradbury, Matheson, and Harlan Ellison. Writing that first novel, *Ghost Road Blues,* made me fall in love with the form, and I now wish I'd started fiction much earlier.

The 'study course' I created for myself involved taking the novels in my genre (American Gothic) and reading them first as a reader, then re-reading several times as a writer—looking for the elements of craft that I'd read about in nonfiction writing books and magazines. Voice, pace, figurative and descriptive language, motif, etc. Not to copy anyone's style, but to understand how contemporary masters of the craft worked their magic. Those novels included '*Salem's Lot* by Stephen King, *Ghost Story* by Peter Straub, *They Thirst* by Robert McCammon, *The Haunting of Hill House* by Shirley Jackson, and a handful of others.

At this writing—July 2021—I'm now working on my 41st novel, and have written more than 125 shorter works, as well as five more nonfiction books about folklore and horror pop culture (under my own name this time), as well as comic books. I now define myself as a novelist, and with a strong and obvious bias toward horror.

MMM: The Bram Stoker Awards are just about the highest honors a horror writer can get. How does it feel to be a five-time winner?

MABERRY: I won my first Stoker for *Ghost Road Blues*, and that shocked the living hell out of me. I was startled to be nominated and stunned to win for *Best First Novel*. Talk about validation! Winning four more crosses over into the territory of surrealism. I have those trophies—the creepy little haunted houses—on a shelf over my published works and it still feels unreal.

MMM: You've published over forty novels, an extensive number of short stories, comic books, and other works. You've shared your knowledge as a writing teacher and lecturer. Netflix adapted *V-Wars* into a series. A number of your novels are in development for various television projects. What's coming up in the future from the magical mind of Jonathan Maberry?

MABERRY: I've got a ton of new material in various stages of development. I'm continuing the Joe Ledger series, of course; but I've closed deals on several other series. I'm co-writing (with Weston Ochse) *Sleepers,* a new military science fiction series. I have the first in a new epic fantasy series, *Kagen the Damned*, scheduled for spring/summer 2022, and am working on the sequel. That had strong support from Michael Moorcock who wrote: "Mr Maberry's first venture into Sword and Sorcery fiction employs powerful imagery to tell a classic tale of revenge and blood which fans of Howard, Moore and Wagner will relish! As his own story grows deeper and more complex, Kagen of Argentium discovers the bizarre answers to more than one mystery. He fights with magnificent skill and fury to restore an empire, unearth the secrets of unimaginably ancient peoples and discovers the horrifying truth behind his family's betrayal. Maberry gradually expands his story until it flows beyond the borders of his chosen genre to create something rich and original. If you hunger for more George Martin, this novel will thoroughly satisfy you. And if you love Lovecraft, you're in for something very special!" Considering that I've been reading his work since I was eight, that hit me very hard. As important to me as a person, as well as a writer, are the cover quotes from Ray Bradbury and Richard Matheson for *Ghost Road Blues.*

I'm also writing a series of shorter science fiction novels that will be prequels to a recent popular science fiction movie, but all details are under NDA for now. And there are other projects in development that will take me into all sorts of creative directions.

MMM: What is the best advice another writer gave to you?

MABERRY: Ray Bradbury told me, "Don't just write the book you want to read . . . write the book you would go out of your way to track down and read. Write that book. Write it with that level of passion and enthusiasm."

MMM: If you could be a monster, which monster would you be and why?

MABERRY: I seldom identify or sympathize with the monsters. I'm more of a fan of the monster hunters. That said, there is one that is a bit of both—the *benandanti*, a werewolf subtype that was popular in Italy centuries ago. These were people who claimed to turn into werewolves as they dreamed, and in that form, they would hunt for evil monsters. I love the idea of a good guy monster, and I based my Sam Hunter private eye on that species. When he takes on a client, he essentially accepts them into his 'pack', and he will do anything to protect his pack.

MMM: Do you have more of a sense of humor than your readers might realize?

JONATHAN MABERRY: There's a lot of humor in my fiction, even the darkest stuff. I laugh a lot and crack jokes and that creeps into my fiction. The thing, though, is that my Joe Ledger character is considerably funnier than I am, which I don't quite understand.

MMM: Last words?

MABERRY: For writers, make sure you learn the business side of publishing as enthusiastically as you learn the elements of craft. Don't be afraid to go outside of your comfort zone and take creative risks.

For nonwriters reading this, if you think you know horror, keep reading . . . it's a much bigger world, with scores of subgenres. There is something for everyone and magic everywhere you look.

And . . . find me on social media
(www.jonathanmaberry.com),
Instagram and Twitter @jonathanmaberry;
Facebook www.facebook.com/jonathanmaberry

> *"The world is filled with things we don't understand. Things that worry us, scare us, endanger us, trouble us. It's always been that way."*
>
> —Elizabeth Massie

SHADOW DREAMS
ELIZABETH MASSIE

BY MICHAEL MCCARTY & DAVID KEMPF

ELIZABETH MASSIE IS a two-time Bram Stoker award-winning author of horror novels, and short fiction. She is an eighth generation Virginian and has been writing professionally since 1984 after her story "Whittler" was published by David B. Silva's "The Horror Show" magazine.

Her horror novels and short story collections include *Sineater, Hell Gate, Desper Hollow, Wire Mesh Mothers, Homeplace, Afraid, It, Watching, Naked on the Edge,* and more. She has written media tie-in books for *Buffy the Vampire Slayer* and *Dark Shadows*.

Her first novel, *Sineater*, and her novella "Stephen" have both won Bram Stoker Awards from the Horror Writers Association. Her *Tudors* novelization (Season 3) won the Scribe Award.

She, along with Mark Rainey, is currently working on *Ameri-Scares* (Crossroad Press) a 50-novel series of spooky books for middle grade readers (age 8-12), a series which was optioned for television by Warner Horizon.

MORE MODERN MYTHMAKERS: The Bram Stoker Awards are just about the highest honors a horror writer can get. How does it feel to be a two-time winner? What does the award mean to you?

ELIZABETH MASSIE: It's an honor to be noted in such a way. There are so many amazing horror writers out there, that to have something identified with an award such as the Stoker is pretty incredible. It's affirming, and it's also something that makes me (or probably any writer) want to do their best with each subsequent story or novel. Not everything we write will be a gem, of course, but I don't mind having something to try to live up to.

MMM: If you could be a monster, which monster would you be and why?

MASSIE: Ha! Interesting question! I suppose I'd like to be a ghost so I could pass through walls, listen in on private conversations, and scare people who need a good shock to the old system. And I love haunted houses, so how cool to live in one of those and actually be part of the haunting? Boo, you!

MMM: You've written books set in the *Buffy the Vampire* and *Dark Shadows* universes. How do you make their universe your own?

MASSIE: That's really not a hard thing to do, if you've been a fan all along. In particular *Dark Shadows* was part of my youth, and oh! did I love that show. I had a crush on Quentin (the handsome character who was also a werewolf) and liked to imagine I was Victoria Winters (the governess at the spooky Collinwood estate). When you've already used your imagination to immerse yourself in a particular fictional universe, it's not all that hard to reclaim those feelings and memories and create a story set right there.

MMM: What are your cures for writer's block?

MASSIE: Some folks say writer's block is a myth, others say it's real. I'm of the "it's real" belief because of course, creativity can be stifled for a variety of reasons. This is true for lots of folks in the creative arts: painters, composers, poets, designers, choreographers, and so on. Everyday life can do that to us. I've certainly had my share of frustratingly dry spells in which I feel stymied and flat; times when I just can't get revved up again to start writing. I have no actual cure, but what I've come up with is a method that helps prevent writer's block. At the end of a writing day, I make a point of stopping in the middle of a scene, or even in the middle of a sentence (and never at the end of a chapter!) It's even better if the scene or sentence is an exciting one. That way, when I pick up again the next morning, I'm already in the throes of some thrilling (and often frightening) adventure. I'm not at a brand-new starting point from which I've got to launch my brain. This method usually works well.

MMM: Tell us more about the *Ameri-Scares* series. How did it start, what is it about?

MASSIE: As I kid, I was drawn to stories of all kinds, in particular scary stories. Our elementary school had those awesome Alfred Hitchcock storybooks for younger readers, and they were a favorite. I also sought out *Tales from the Crypt* and the Gold Key *Twilight Zone* comic books. They both frightened and fascinated me. Perfect!

When I started writing in earnest (as in for publication),

I aimed at the adult market. Very few if any regulations or restrictions when your audience is mature. And I love writing with a completely free hand. Yet, as a horror-loving kid from way back as well as a mom and a former middle school science teacher (19 years in the classroom), I also wanted to create something for younger readers, as well. I loved the idea of a series. A nice BIG series with much to offer!

So, what could be a bigger series than one in which each state in the union was the basis of a novel? I mean, 50 at least, right, and with the option to go back through each state if the series grew to be that large? The horror fan in me wanted these novels to be appropriately spooky, but not graphic, and terrifying, with strong main characters with whom readers would identify and exciting plots that would give readers the chills I remember loving so very much at that age. I also liked the idea of having a touch of educational value (!) to the books . . . Each novel is based on or inspired by an actual folktale, legend, or true historic event from the state in which the story is set. That way, readers might even decide to investigate those legends or events and learn more about them on their own. And so, *Ameri-Scares* was born.

So far, there are 12 novels in the series—Virginia, West Virginia, Maryland, North Carolina, Tennessee, New York, Illinois, Ohio, Michigan, California, Montana, and Washington. With more on the horizon! Author Mark Rainey has joined me in this venture, and he's contributed some fantastic books! And we've found that adults seem to enjoy these novels as much as middle graders do. Quick, spooky, fun reads that will take you back to your youth.

MMM: Which book was the easiest to write and which book was the most difficult and why?

MASSIE: None have been easy to write, though if I was pressed for an "easiest" I would say *Sineater* or *Desper*

Hollow. (We're talking novels here, not any of my many collections of short fiction.) That's because both are set in an area of the country, Appalachia, with which I'm very familiar. I live in the Shenandoah Valley of Virginia, right next to the Appalachian chain, and my family has been in this region since the mid-1700s. It's "in my blood" as they say. I'm not a hillbilly. I'm not a mountain girl. But I know the hills. I know the mountains. I know many of the people. Both *Sineater* and *Desper Hollow* spring from mountain legends and mysterious mountain practices, though I make them my own. My characters are not cardboard hill-folk cutouts. They are recognizable and often sympathetic human beings faced with supernatural or imagined supernatural dangers and do their best to survive.

The most difficult would probably be *Hell Gate*, though I loved the writing and loved the results. This novel is set in Coney Island at the turn of the 20th century, and the research for this was extensive. I didn't mind—I'm a huge fan of old amusement parks because of the eerie, glaring, dangerous, fantastically wonderful mystery to be found there. Not only did I need the research for the physical location (Dreamland, Steeplechase Park, Luna Park), but I needed to learn about females in law enforcement at that time and how they were seen and treated. *Hell Gate* took almost two years to complete. It was worth it.

MMM: When did you first become interested in writing?

MASSIE: I've been a storyteller ever since I can remember. When I was a little girl, I was constantly entertaining (I use that term lightly; who knows how entertained they really were?) my family with made up "what if" tales. At night I might ask my mother, "What if when we're sleeping a ghost comes down the chimney?" Or in the car with my dad, when we would stop to fill the tank with gasoline, I might say, "See that cute little stray dog over there? What if I opened the car door and he got in with us and wouldn't get out?" Of course, then I'd launch off that question and explain all the things that might happen based on my scenario.

My parents were very patient and encouraging, though. In fact, my dad, the president of our hometown newspaper, had a lot to do with sealing my desire to be a writer. One evening, when I was four, I made up and shared a story about a squirrel who had lost her favorite acorn. When I went to bed, my father drove down to the newspaper office, typed up (yes, this was in the day of typewriters!) my story, as best as he could remember, found clip art of squirrels in one of the big advertising books, and hand-bound it into a booklet with a really cute cover. The next morning, he gave it to me. I was thrilled that I could now read and re-read (I was reading by the time I was four) my story and share it with others. I'm sure my parents' eyes glazed over with my twentieth reading, but I didn't notice at the time.

MMM: How did you get involved in horror?

MASSIE: I watched the original *The Twilight Zone* and original *The Outer Limits* on television as a kid. Scared me to death, but I couldn't get enough. I think the reason is this . . . the characters were, for the most part, people I could care about. These characters faced frightening and often overwhelming situations . . . sometimes they made it out okay, other times they didn't. And so, early on, it impressed on me the fact that horror, done well, could create and encourage sympathy and empathy. I really liked that. Also, these two shows tackled social issues that were often ignored during that time period. That was another big plus for me, another aspect of horror that steered me in its direction.

MMM: What are some of your favorite horror books?

MASSIE: Oh, so many! Must I really narrow them down? Okay, I'll list some of the all-time favorites, but keep in mind there are others!

The Stand by Stephen King
Harvest Home by Thomas Tryon
Behind Her Eyes by Sarah Pinborough
The Bank by Bentley Little
The Good House by Tananarive Due
Midnight Sun by Ramsey Campbell
The Drive-In by Joe Lansdale
Rebecca by Daphne Du Maurier
Innocence by Dean Koontz
Deathwatch by Lisa Mannetti

I'd recommend anyone who has missed any of these to hide themselves and post haste to the nearest bookstore (brick and mortar or online) and grab a copy.

MMM: What are some of your favorite horror movies?

MASSIE: While *The Exorcist* (1973, based on the William Peter Blatty novel) may be dated now, I remember being utterly terrified and enthralled by how well the movie told the story. The lighting, the pacing, the slowly encroaching and then in-your-face terror was near-perfect. No real gore except for the vomit, but it didn't need gore. Though I'm not a devil-believer, this film came close to changing my mind!

The Other, a 1972 film based on Thomas Tryon's novel of the same name (and not to be confused with the 2001 film, *The Others*), was another movie that I'll never forget and count as a favorite. It doesn't shove the viewer's face into a shitload of blood and guts but is subtle and dark and creepy as hell. The ending is at once horrifying and heartbreaking.

1939's *The Dark Eyes of London* (stupidly renamed *The Human Monster* here in the States) is one I saw initially as a child on television. I didn't really understand all that was going on, but I was both frightened by the evil man in charge of the blind institute, and so very sad for the hapless, doomed characters in the film.

The Thing (1982) has all the suspense and payoff that any horror lover would look for. Isolated, claustrophobic setting and characters struggling to figure out what the hell is trying to kill them. Not a lot of gore, but shocking scenes, nonetheless.

Get Out (a 2017 gem from Jordan Peele), does a brilliant job of revealing the horror of racism in a unique and horrifying way.

I could go on, there are many other favorite films; but I will point out that I'll always prefer a movie with a good, strong story, with characters I care about, with horror that picks up the pace and does so without relying on relentless, graphic violence (I'm not a big fan of films like the *Hostel* and *Saw* franchises), and stays away from jump scares and screeching, pop-your-eardrums music.

MMM: What is your opinion of the self-publishing trend?

MASSIE: It was inevitable, given the way large, traditional publishing houses are buying up other publishers, shrinking the market, and making it more difficult for newer writers to get picked up. Writers who create what the publishing houses determine to be blockbusters are now paid even more bucks than before, which leaves less money for B-list (and I think B-list is really tight now, too, and possibly dying). All this makes it even more difficult for newer writers to break in. And so, self-publishing is a route many new . . . and some established . . . authors are taking. There are some fantastic self-published works, and I'm glad writers have taken the reins when no one else would. And self-published books shouldn't be judged solely on the fact that they are self-published.

That said, there is a ton of self-published garbage out

there . . . Works that should never have been put up for sale in the first place because they are nothing more than self-indulgent ramblings, or good intentions with bad grammar, weak plots, or cardboard characters. This makes it more difficult for those with good, solid stories out there.

Little anecdote: I had an appointment with a new eye doctor a couple months ago. She didn't know me, just had my eye chart from the earlier doctor. As she was getting ready to check my vision, she said, "So, what do you do?" I said, "I'm a writer." She chuckled and said, "Yeah, during the pandemic everybody's at home now, writing books." That struck hard. But she was right in many ways, though it isn't just the current coronavirus pandemic that has set more people onto the "publishing" path. It seems that many want to claim they are writers but aren't willing to put the solid work into creating something worth reading. So, to make a long answer short (too late), I'll say I have no idea what publishing will be like in the next two, five, ten years, be it through traditional houses, smaller presses, or self-publishing. I can only hope that people keep reading, and that good writers will continue to share their talents and their visions. I'm counting on them, because, c'mon, I wanna READ!

MMM: Do you have any advice for new writers?

MASSIE: Read as much as you can, not just in your chosen genre. Realize that not everything you write will be a gem; a lot will suck, and that's okay. First drafts are first drafts, not final drafts; find a good editor and give serious consideration to the suggestions that editor gives you. When you start a new story or novel, have an idea of where you want your story to end up, so at least you have a sense of direction; this doesn't mean things won't change as you write, but it will keep you from grinding to a halt, standing in the middle of the road, wondering which way to turn.

Don't get pissed if your work gets bad reviews . . . press on and try to do better with the next one. Please, unless you are a skilled, trained illustrator, don't draw or paint your own book cover. (Have you seen how many awful book covers are out there? It's painful!) Write most days but give yourself time away to let your creative well refill . . . and it will.

MMM: Why do you think horror books remain so popular?

MASSIE: The world is filled with things we don't understand. Things that worry us, scare us, endanger us, trouble us. It's always been that way. Horror, in particular, has been popular for eons because it gives readers or listeners or viewers a chance to vicariously step in and see how others might handle a terrifying situation, to even imagine how they might deal with that same situation. It's like a test run, not that many of us will ever actually encounter zombies or werewolves or vampires. However, many of us (most if not all of us) will run into things that scare the shit out of us. It's good to know we're not the only ones. Plus, I think that, as I say in the introduction of my now OOP collection, *Sundown*, we "stare into the darkness to better understand the light."

"I've always done my best for the development of characters and they have always been shaped by the nature of the story I'm after. The environment might come first, or a question might come first or a puzzle might come first—all of those will shape the characters."

—Larry Niven

TO OUR RINGWORLD'S CHILDREN, CHILDREN, CHILDREN

LARRY NIVEN

LARRY NIVEN IS one of the best writers in the field of Hard Science Fiction (fiction very much grounded in science, mathematics, and physics). Born on April 30, 1938 in Los Angeles, he graduated with a Bachelor of Arts in mathematics from Washburn University, Kansas in 1962 and completed one year of graduate work at UCLA before dropping out to write.

In 1964 he sold his first short story "The Coldest Place" for the sum of $25.00 to *Worlds of If* magazine. His next three stories, "World Of Ptavvs" were published in *Worlds of Tomorrow*, "Wrong-Way Street" and "One Face" both appeared *Galaxy*. All these magazines were edited by sci-fi legend Frederik Pohl (who was interviewed in the ebook edition of *Modern Mythmakers: 35 Interviews with Horror & Science Fiction Writers and Filmmakers*).

Niven's first novel was an expansion of his short story *World Of Ptavvs* in 1966. He also penned such classics as *The Integral Trees, Footfall, Destiny's Road,* and *The Mote Of God's Eye* (co-written with Jerry Pournelle). Recent publications include the books *Glorious* (with Gregory Benford), *The Seascape Tattoo,* and the short story collection *Madness From The Inconstant Moon.*

Besides books, he has also written scripts for TV series such as the original *Land of the Lost, Star Trek: The Animated Series,* and the 1995 *Outer Limits* with "Inconstant Moon" (a story about a physics professor that realized the sun has gone nova and mankind only has a few hours to live, and spends the final hours courting a woman he secretly loved).

He is the author of the series *Ringworld* (which has won a Hugo, a Nebula, a Ditmar in Australia, Locust and a Daicon in Japan), *The Ringworld Engineers, The Ringworld Throne, Ringworld's Children,* and *Fate of Worlds.*

Besides winning multiple Hugo awards and the Nebula, he has won the Robert Heinlein Award, The Edward E. Smith Memorial Award, and a Prometheus Award.

MORE MODERN MYTHMAKERS: Did you ever imagine that *Ringworld* would still be popular after fifty years? What do you think contributes to the novel's popularity?

LARRY NIVEN: After it was published and after it was having some success, then I could imagine it would last fifty years and more. When I was writing it, I wondered if anyone would take it seriously, the size of the structure was way outside the limits I've seen in hard science fiction (1 million miles wide and 600 million miles long). There had been soft science fiction that had dealt with things bigger, such as *Cosmic Engineers* by Clifford Simak; I read when I was a kid.

What I was after was to present this huge structure and make people believe in it, and I did my damndest to do that. I had my doubts until it hit print and started getting good reviews and winning awards.

MMM: Freeman Dyson introduced the concept of the "Dyson Sphere" in the early 1960's, was this theory influential in your *Ringworld* series?

NIVEN: Yes, definitely. Freedom Dyson conceived the "Dyson Shell," the notion of the "Dyson Shell" is a successful civilization will eventually need all the output of its star, it will have to enter up all the sunlight of a star in order to use it for industrial purposes. You'll wind up looking at a much bigger object, a shell of anything, radiating heat about the temperature of warm water, that is if it is built by things remotely resembling humans or Earthly life. That is the "Dyson Shell."

The "Dyson Sphere" is taking the idea to an extreme, building a giant Ping-Pong ball outside of a star—93 million miles in radius, again if they resemble Earthly life.

I looked at the Ping-Pong ball and started redesigning; there is no way to get gravity on that Ping-Pong ball. There never used to be, when I was writing. At this point, dark energy seems to promise that we can have anti-gravity if we really want it—which wasn't true when I was writing *Ringworld*. I put it in anyway, but not in the *Ringworld*.

MMM: What was your inspiration for your Speaker-To-Animals character?

NIVEN: Various writers had written of catlike aliens, villains, and heroes. I made mine a little different and introduced the notion that a reaction drive is a deadly weapon.

MMM: You lived and wrote for the most part of the 20th century. Now we are in the 21st century. What do you think of humanity's prospects in the 21st century and beyond? Where do you think the world is heading from here?

NIVEN: I didn't see the coronavirus coming. I favor the notion of an oncoming Ice Age, which I expect we can survive with style—and solar power. Geothermal plants in Yellowstone Park would help that survival, relieving pressure that would otherwise wipe out the west coast and more.

MMM: You've done a number of collaborations with the late, great Jerry Pournelle. What is the secret of your success with this collaboration?

NIVEN: Mutual respect. I've written a couple articles on collaborations. Mutual respect is one of the secrets. One of you has to have the veto power, or you can get stalled in the middle of something. When we first started, Jerry and I agreed one of us would rewrite the novel from the beginning to smooth out discrepancies in style, you don't want jarring changes in style in a novel. The one who was going to do that work on the first novel (*The Mote In God's Eye*) was going to be Jerry. In the second novel (*Inferno*) it was me.

With *Inferno* it took us four months to write. Most of our novels take two to four years.

MMM: Talking about *Inferno*, in the sequel, *Escape From Hell*, your character Allen Carpenter literally escapes from the underworld. In his dark adventures he encounters several deceased individuals such as Sylvia Plath, Lester del Rey, Anna Nicole Smith, Carl Sagan, J. Edgar Hoover, Leon Trotsky, and several others. How did you and Jerry Pournelle decide whom to choose as characters in hell? Were there any concerns of lawsuits? Did you get permission from the estates?

NIVEN: We got no permissions. The lawsuits (and outright riots) we avoided are not visible. Jerry was well read compared to me, so most of the characters Carpenter saw were Jerry's.

MMM: *In Lucifer's Hammer* (co-written with Jerry Pournelle) the protagonist Tim Hammer, who first sights the comet, is blamed for the terrible things that happen to Earth. Do you see him as an example of the classic outsider?

NIVEN: Yes. In fact, Tim Hammer, as he came out, is Jerry Pournelle's version of what I'm like. I didn't fiddle because much of what Jerry's version of what I'm like is an interesting character (laughs).

MMM: What do you think are the main preoccupations with Science Fiction these days?

NIVEN: Political correctness. As a writer I've noticed that a series always devolves into politics, no matter how you fight it. It's bad to start with politics.

MMM: In earlier works, your background in mathematics played a noticeable role in the storyline—for example: the physics involved in the practical use of teleportation devices (alibi machines) or moving about the *Integral Trees* on the rim of *Ringworld*. In later works, the stories took a more transparent role, imposing their rules by nature. What effect does character development have on how vivid the world will be?

NIVEN: I've always done my best for the development of characters and they have always been shaped by the nature of the story I'm after. The environment might come first, or a question might come first, or a puzzle might come first—

all of those will shape the characters. I've always done my best to shape them to reality, I feel best when my characters start to act for themselves.

MMM: Talking about characters, the Gil Hamilton series of short stories was always a fun read. How is Gil, and what has he been up to lately?

NIVEN: I like those stories very much too, but they are hard to write. I have a bunch of notes for Gil, but I don't have any further stories. There are only five so far. If I could come up with a notion, I'd write one, but if I don't, I can't.

MMM: How do you maintain an active fascination for science fiction?

NIVEN: It is very easy to maintain an active attraction for science—because the sciences have been so active themselves; new discoveries everywhere. Once upon a time, Isaac Asimov wrote an article about the difficulty of keeping up with the science field. If he was writing today, his problem today would be—he could keep up, but so could every yahoo. The internet can tell you everything. That is how I keep up with the sciences.

How do I keep an interest in science fiction? There are some good writers out there, is the answer.

MMM: On the same line, who are some of your favorite genre writers?

NIVEN: In fantasy, I like Terry Pratchett, he got my attention pretty quickly—one of his first novels, *Strata,* was a pastiche of *Ringworld*. In science fiction, I've read a lot of Stephen Baxter's books—I'm not caught up with him like I am with Pratchett.

MMM: Do you think we'll get a manned mission to Mars in our lifetimes?

NIVEN: Well, I'm 82. How old are you?

MMM: I'm 50-something.

NIVEN: Maybe yes for you, but no for me. Mars is tough, Mars is tougher than the moon, and we can't get to the moon. If we can put a man on the moon, why can't we put a man on the moon?

MMM: Do you mean like a colony on the moon?

NIVEN: We can't reach the moon at all today; it is already a part of the past. People born on the day we reached the moon and the last day we reached the moon are already middle aged.

(Author's note, the next scheduled mission to the moon is 2024).

MMM: Today, what recent discoveries or advancements in science amaze you?

NIVEN: There has been a lot of wonderful stuff. Dark matter, dark energy—were getting more answers to these puzzles. The puzzles didn't exist, as far as I'm concerned, until recently.

Games played with light speed, you can slow light down, and you can stop light in its tracks and restart it.

The Hubble is still at work and discovering wonderful things.

What I find scary is, I don't know why I find this scary—it just gets me in the bones. The universe has about 20 billion years to go, by the end of 20 billion years planets—

everything comes apart and then atoms come apart, then subatomic particles come apart. All pulled apart by dark energy, getting stronger and stronger rolling into the other forces of the universe. I find that an unpleasant picture.

MMM: What kinds of things do you do to relax?

NIVEN: I do yoga, I hike, and I play racquetball with a partner named Peggy Little, who can only get loose on Friday evenings because she works for a living.

MMM: The term "Tales Of Known Space" is used to describe your early work. What does that phrase mean?

NIVEN: I worked it out like this: known space is the volume which is known—that we know something about having sent probes or ships through it. Human space is the volume controlled by human beings. They both are vague volumes. Most of the space between stars still isn't occupied through Louie Wu's (protagonist from Niven's short stories and *Ringworld*) time. Known space is a future you understand running from several years ago through 3100.

Robert Heinlein did the first future history to be named one. It looked like a fun thing to do for a lot of us.

MMM: Was it *The Mote In God's Eye* that Robert Heinlein said was one of his favorite science fiction books?

NIVEN: Yes.

MMM: How did that make you feel? Was that a real high in your career at that point?

NIVEN: Yes it was, it was definitely a high in our career— my career and Jerry's too. What Robert (Heinlein) did when Jerry imposed upon him to read our manuscript was, he said, "If you make certain changes this will be the best science fiction book that I have ever read." We looked his changes over and argued about it and then made them and that was the first time that had ever happened to Robert—but now he was committed, he did a full proofreading job on *The Mote Of God's Eye* because his reputation was behind it now and death upon our heads if we ever revealed the fact while he was still alive. He didn't want to do that twice (laughs)—let alone 30 or 40 times. He had friends closer than Jerry Pournelle.

That was a high in our careers and a terrific boost and a terrific set of lessons.

MMM: Is your character Alex Griffin (co-created with Steven Barnes) going to have any new adventures in the Dream Park?

NIVEN: Steven Barnes has moved up to the Northwest, not just for years, but decades. We did a little writing together then. But he's moving back into the Los Angeles area—which means it will be easier to collaborate. We want to do a *Dream Park* novel. We haven't gotten into huge detail yet—but we want to do that.

MMM: Last words?

NIVEN: Keep the faith in the future.

"I loved it, but I also took my cameo very seriously (in The Return of the Living Dead*). I never broke character that day—which upset a lot of people. I was originally cast as the shopping cart bum, but our line producer nixed that idea. He thought that as the film's production designer, I already had enough on my plate."*

—William Stout

WORLDS OF WONDER
WILLIAM STOUT

WILLIAM STOUT IS a famously diverse artist of international renown in many fields: entertainment theme and motion picture design (specialized in science fiction/fantasy horror film), comic book art, book illustrations, poster design, CD covers, public murals, and dynamic yet accurate reconstruction of prehistory life. His endeavors in the fields of movies and comics have gained him a loyal following, making him a popular guest at comic book, science fiction, and horror movie conventions around the world.

In 1978, Stout began his film career with the movie *Buck Rogers of the 25th Century.* He has worked on over thirty feature films including *Conan the Barbarian, Conan the Destroyer, The Hitcher,* and the *Invaders From Mars* remake. The cult classic *The Return of the Living Dead* made Stout the youngest production designer in film history. Stout wrote *The Warrior and the Sorceress* for Roger Corman and a dinosaur feature for Jim Henson. He did the production design for the *Masters of the Universe,* and designed the key character for Walt Disney's *Dinosaur* (2000). He designed Edgar (the big bug in *Men In Black*) for ILM in 1996. Stout's other work includes designs for Guillermo del Toro's horror classic *Pan's Labyrinth,* Christopher Nolan's *The Prestige,* and the creatures in Frank Darabont's film of Stephen King's *The Mist.*

During his career in the arts, he has won several awards including the Inkpot Award, and Spectrum Gold and Silver awards. Books that he illustrated also won awards including the Children's Choice Award for *The Little Blue Brontosaurus* by Byron Preiss (the book was the basis for the 1988 animated feature *The Land Before Time*) and Richard Matheson's *Adu & The 7 Marvels* won the Society of Illustrators Gold and Silver medal awards, and the Benjamin Franklin award.

MORE MODERN MYTHMAKERS: How did you go from underground comic book artist to working in the cinema?

WILLIAM STOUT: I accidentally fell into the film business. Ironically, I've found the more you want to work in film, the harder it is to get a job in that business.

My friend Bob Greenberg was working as a production assistant on *Conan the Barbarian.* I had no interest in making movies at that time; I was making a fortune advertising them. But I was a big Robert E. Howard/*Conan* fan. Bob told me Ron Cobb was the production designer. That blew my mind, because I only knew Cobb as a political cartoonist for the underground newspapers. I was intrigued. What would he do with *Conan?*

I wanted to come by the *Conan* offices to see what he was doing, but I just didn't have the time—I was too busy creating movie posters.

I finally got a break from my schedule—but instead of going to the *Conan* offices, I went to the ABA (American Booksellers Association) event at the Los Angeles Convention Center. The ABA was a great place for an illustrator to pick up work, as every single editor and publisher in America was there.

The first person I ran into at the ABA was, coincidentally, Ron Cobb. He told me that I was his first choice of whom to work with on *Conan*. But, he explained, he had a deal with John Milius, the film's director. John had veto-power over anyone Ron wanted to hire. Would I be so kind as to drop off my portfolio for John to see? I went to the *Conan* offices the next day. Kathleen Kennedy was the receptionist. Milius happened to be there. I met with John. He flipped through my samples portfolio, recognized a *Heavy Metal* story I had done that he had liked and handed me back my book. As he walked out the door, he barked "Hire him!"

I then had a meeting with Buzz Feitshans, the line producer. He told me what I would be making on *Conan*. I nearly fell off my chair laughing. It was 10% of what I was making in advertising! Nevertheless, I thought it might be fun to learn how films were made. Plus, the job was only for two weeks. Well, the two weeks turned into two years—and a film career. Oh, and whose office was opposite mine when I started on *Conan*?—Steven Spielberg. Cobb and I would work on *Conan* during the day and then at 6:00 PM cross the hall into Steven's office where we would kick around ideas for Steven's next film project, *Raiders of the Lost Ark*.

MMM: You've done storyboards for such films as *First Blood*, *The Return of the Living Dead*, *Raiders of the Lost Ark* (uncredited) and other movies too. Explain the process that goes into doing a storyboard.

STOUT: First, I read the script. Then, if possible, I talk to the director. I want to know what his vision is for the film. If he doesn't have one (some directors are just not very visual), then I feel it's my job (working in tandem with the production designer) to help create one. Then, I either board the entire film or, most commonly, board the key scenes of the movie, the action scenes, the effects scenes or the most difficult to visually understand scenes.

MMM: Is there anything cut from one of your storyboards, you wished they kept for any film?

STOUT: I wish they had kept the entrance I had designed for Evil-Lyn in *Masters of the Universe*. I think main character entrances and their design are very important. They can tell you so much about the character without anyone saying a word.

MMM: What are the things you are most proud of with your storyboards?

STOUT: Their strong composition and the clarity of their storytelling.

MMM: I like to talk a little about the film *The Return of the Living Dead* because I feel this is such a watershed film with zombie motion pictures. As far as I know, it is the first movie that featured fast moving zombies, which is done a lot nowadays. Why do you think this movie has been such a hit with audiences for over three decades now?

STOUT: It accomplished something that's very difficult to pull off: it was very scary AND very funny. And the humor didn't come from jokes—it was funny because (like the great beginnings of John Landis' *An American Werewolf in London* and *Twilight Zone: The Movie*) of the characters' natural, real life responses to horrific situations.

The characters also seem to be true friends with a real past together. That was mainly due to Dan O'Bannon's gift to the cast of two weeks of rehearsal prior to shooting.

MMM: In *The Return of the Living Dead*, you play a bum towards the beginning of the movie. How was it to be on the other side of the camera for a change?

STOUT: I loved it, but I also took my cameo very seriously. I never broke character that day—which upset a lot of people. I was originally cast as the shopping cart bum but our line producer nixed that idea. He thought that as the film's production designer, I already had enough on my plate.

MMM: In *The Return of the Living Dead*, there is this half lady corpse that is strapped onto a steel table and slapping her spinal cord around and she is leaking spinal fluid. Do you remember what they used for the spinal fluid? Did you also help with the production of that scene?

STOUT: I'm a hands-on production designer. For that scene I was under the gurney, operating the mechanism that made the spine flop around and ooze spinal fluid, while Tony Gardner operated her arms, and Brian Peck (Scuzz) puppeteered her head and mouth. Brian also spoke her lines for the temp track (which later got replaced with a female voice).

I don't know what was used for the spinal fluid. I would guess it was glycerin. You'll have to ask Tony Gardner for the definitive answer to that question.

MMM: In *The Return of the Living Dead*, one of the characters is reading one of your comic books in the backseat of the car. Which comic book are they reading?

STOUT: Scuzz is reading *Weird Trips*—the Ed Gein issue. Ed (the inspiration for *Psycho*'s Norman Bates) died during the making of our film. Dan O'Bannon and I had a moment of silence for old Ed when we got the news.

MMM: Have any other of your comics ended up on the silver screen?

STOUT: Not that I know of . . .

MMM: You've done a number of famous movie posters as well, including *Wizards*, *House*, *Life of Brian*, *More American Graffiti* and *Up From the Depths*. First of all, they are fantastic pop art. How do you go about capturing an entire film with just one image of artwork?

STOUT: I either watch the movie, read the script or ask my advertising art director for some direction. Then, I make a list of what I consider all of the most important elements of the film. I then try combining some of them to create an arresting image that somehow captures the feeling of the movie at its most moving or exciting.

MMM: You did a comic book of *King Kong*. *King Kong* is an iconic movie monster of over eighty years. What are some of your favorite *Kong* movies over the years?

STOUT: The original 1933 classic is my favorite movie of all time. I have a soft spot for the rushed-to-the-screen sequel, *Son of Kong*, too. I think all the other *Kong* films are crap, quite honestly.

MMM: Did you feel a lot of pressure in doing the *Kong* covers, because you were doing the artwork of one of the most famous monsters in cinema?

STOUT: No; it was sheer, total pleasure on my part; I was in my element. I wanted to do all of the covers but they only let me do two.

MMM: You also have connections with the *Godzilla* world. You wrote the episode "Why is thy Sting" for the animated *Godzilla: The Series* which pits The King of the Monsters against a gigantic mutated scorpion called Ts-eh-go. How did you get that gig?

STOUT: My animation agent, John Goldsmith, scored that gig for me. It was a tremendous experience. Animation writers are treated SO differently from movie screenwriters. It felt like I was living in Fantasyland.

MMM: What did you think of the show?

STOUT: I was very impressed. Except for me, they had top professional writers turning in scripts with terrific characters and dialogue. The writers were inspired by the quality of Joss Whedon's *Buffy The Vampire Slayer* TV series—and it showed. Nice look, too.

MMM: Of all the *Godzilla* films, which are your favorite?

STOUT: I know this sounds like sacrilege but, honestly, I'm not a real big fan of the *Godzilla* movies. I think the suits look hokey. They're baggy and you can always tell that there's a guy inside. The early ones in the series are painfully slow. There's a lot of unintentional humor in most Kaiju movies. I really like Toho's *Attack of the Mushroom People*, though. It pissed me off that the Matthew Broderick *Godzilla* movie kept repeating effects (a big no-no in the Stout filmmaking handbook). The new big budget *Godzilla* movie hardly had Godzilla in it at all.

My favorite is the one we didn't get to make.

MMM: *Pan's Labyrinth*, you were a conceptual artist for the film. What did you contribute to the movie?

STOUT: I created the first designs for the Faun (Pan), the exterior of the main set (the building that houses the general, the girl and her mother), the giant toad (originally it was going to be carved from stone. It had all kinds of runes and symbols covering its body), and something we called the Nerve Ghost, a creepy character that got cut from the film.

MMM: What was it like working with Guillermo del Toro?

STOUT: Guillermo gave me good direction and a lot of freedom. I wish he could have afforded me for the entire film.

MMM: On a related note, Guillermo del Toro was supposed to make a movie of H.P. Lovecraft's *At the Mountains of Madness*. What has ever happened to that project? Were you going to be involved with *Mountains* too?

STOUT: Guillermo told me he wanted the triumvirate of Mike Mignola, Wayne Barlowe and me to design the film. The project seemed like it was on the verge of being made a number of times. Then, something would come up (like *Pacific Rim*), and it would be postponed and kicked down the road for another chunk of time. Guillermo also was insistent that the film to be a hard R-rated movie. The studios didn't think that would pencil out financially.

MMM: Do you do a series of studies before beginning a project?

STOUT: Always. My first advertising course at art school was taught by the Boston brothers. They were tough. I had them on Tuesdays and Thursdays. On Tuesday they would assign us two ads to do for Thursday. We were expected to show 200 thumbnail ideas for each ad. On Thursday, we were assigned four ads. Same thing: 200 thumbnails per ad. So, that resulted in my coming up with 1200 ideas and sketches—plus the six ads themselves—per week for that class, in addition to all the work I was assigned in my other classes. I'm glad that class was in my first semester at art school. It made the rest of my four years seem like a piece of cake.

MMM: What mediums do you use?

STOUT: My favorite medium is oil on canvas. I rarely use that medium in film, however, as it is too slow for movie work (even though I use fast drying oils—alkyds—when I paint) and I need to work outside (because of the fumes).
    I also enjoy pen & ink, watercolor, ink & watercolor and acrylic painting (somewhat; acrylics have several disadvantages, most notably that it dries about 10% darker than what you put down). I color my comics digitally now (I used to cut hand separations and then later used the European gouache-on-blue-line method). I'm a decent sculptor, but I rarely sculpt because I am so damned slow at it—unlike when I work graphically.

MMM: How long does it take before you are satisfied with the results?

STOUT: That varies piece-to-piece. Complex works take longer for obvious reasons. Typically, though, a 24" x 18" oil painting takes me about three days. A comic book cover usually takes me a day to pencil (more if I'm doing all the cover lettering), two thirds of a day to ink and a day to color.

My pen & ink convention sketches typically take an hour or two.

MMM: What advice would you give to someone who wants to be an artist?

STOUT: Do as much life (figure) drawing as possible, and never stop (on the days you can't find a model, draw yourself in a good full length mirror). One day per week should be devoted to animal drawing from life (pets, zoo, neighborhood animals). If you want to be a painter, do some plein air painting (on-the-spot landscape painting) as much as you can. It will teach you color, design, composition and how to handle your paint. Always give 100%, no matter how much or how little you're being paid for the job. Your past will never come back to haunt you, and you'll get better as an artist at a faster rate. Plus, your clients will be pleased.

MMM: What advice would you give to someone who wants to work in the film industry?

STOUT: Don't, it will break your heart. The most often question I get asked now on films is, "Bill . . . you're a really nice guy. What are you doing in the film business?"

That should tell you something. It's a brutal business, especially for women. I have successfully persuaded many of my family members not to get into The Biz. I think they're much happier for taking my advice.

If you're single and can't do anything else, then go for it. If you're in a relationship, however, expect it to be destroyed. The divorce rate on David Lynch's *Dune* was 95%. There were people in that picture who hadn't seen their families in six years.

If you're doing your job properly on a film, you should be working 18-hour days, seven days a week minimum. I promise you will dearly earn every penny that you make.

MMM: Of all the movies you've done, which ones are you the most satisfied with?

STOUT: *The Return of the Living Dead, Conan the Barbarian*, the opening to Walt Disney's *Dinosaur* (before the dinosaurs talked), our unmade *Godzilla*, Stephen King's *The Mist, Pan's Labyrinth, The Prestige, The Muppets Wizard of Oz* (before it was cast), *Men In Black, Predator* (but with the original ending that was never shot), *Rambling Rose, House, The Hitcher, First Blood, Raiders of the Lost Ark* and the Firesign Theatre movie *Everything You Know Is Wrong*. The trailer for *Monster Roll* (with my creature design) is incredible. *Magic Kingdom* could have been incredible—but the Disney attorneys screwed that one up.

MMM: Which are you the least satisfied with?

STOUT: Easy. *Theodore Rex*, the most expensive direct-to-video movie ever made. To give you an idea how wrong this film was, it starred Whoopi Goldberg in a part written for Val Kilmer. I was the movie's production designer for the first nine months of pre-production. It was the only film I ever walked away from. Leaving that film is one of the reasons I'm still alive. I was disappointed that there weren't more differences between the scripts of *Invaders From Mars* and our remake.

I worked on three different versions of *John Carter of Mars*—but not the one that got made. There was one script I worked on that would have been a terrific film. I'm sorry that the *Conran* brothers didn't get their shot. We had a great vision for their movie.

Ant Bully could have been so much better. I was only on that film for about a week when Warners tried to negate our deal, so I left. Nevertheless, nearly everything I created during that one week made it to the screen.

MMM: Do you have a good behind-the-scenes story you'd like to share?

STOUT: I loved Billy Barty (Gwildor in *Masters of the Universe*). Every morning I'd feel a tug on my coat. I'd turn around and it was Billy. He had a new joke for me every single day on the set. He was such a sweet guy.

MMM: Last words?

STOUT: Find what you love to do and then endeavor to become the best at it. Be your own biggest fan. Give value to your time and work. Stand up for yourself. Expect the industries you work in (and their jobs) to change—because they will.
    And be kind.

"Clowns Vs. Spiders is an all-out horror/comedy, but I wanted both elements to work. If you don't think it's funny, hopefully it's still a great horror novel, and if you don't think it's scary, hopefully you still get a lot of laughs out of it."

—Jeff Strand

DEAD CLOWN BARBECUE
JEFF STRAND

JEFF STRAND IS a Bram Stoker and Splatterpunk Award Winner and the author of over fifty books. Known for his horror novels such as *Pressure, Dweller, My Pretties, Clown Vs. Spiders, Autumn Bleeds into Winter, Benjamin's Parasite, Blister, The Sinister Mr. Corpse,* and the *Wolf Hunt* trilogy. He has also written several young adult books including *A Bad Day for Voodoo, The Greatest Zombie Movie Ever, How You Ruined My Life, Stranger Things Have Happened,* and *I Have a Bad Feeling About This.* Also, the author of the short story collections *Dead Clown Barbecue, Gleefully Macabre Tales,* and *Everything Has Teeth.*

The Writing Life: Reflections, Recollections and a Lot of Cursing is a nonfiction collection of essays on the lessons he learned from writing horror books for a living, such as how to survive bad reviews, rejections from editors, and having a book signing that nobody shows up for. It is a great book for the horror writers and non-horror writers alike.

Strand's primarily known for mixing horror and comedy, even though some of his books are "serious," and some of them aren't horror. Still, he will milk the "No author working today comes close to Jeff Strand's perfect mixture of comedy and terror" quote from Cemetery Dance until the day he dies. Several of his books are in development as motion pictures. He has a very small part in a Herschell Gordon Lewis movie where he gets killed by the Big Bad Wolf.

To learn more about Jeff Strand and his books go to: Http://www.Jeffstrand.com

Subscribe to his free monthly newsletter (which includes a brand-new original short story in every issue) at http://eepurl.com/bpv5br.

MORE MODERN MYTHMAKERS: Were you surprised that your collection of anecdotes about your horror writing in your book *The Writing Life: Reflections, Recollections and a Lot of Cursing* would be very well received (including a rave review in Rue Morgue Magazine)?

JEFF STRAND: I feel like an arrogant douchebag starting off this interview by saying, "No, not at all!" but I put a ton of work into that book with the expectation that people would really like it. I haven't been a newbie in a long time, and I've got stuff to say! I wanted it to be the book equivalent of hanging out in a bar at a writers' conference, or something like Stephen King's *On Writing* where the author hasn't spent the past few decades being rich and famous. It took me a long time to get to where I am, and I still have a long way to go, and I know enough authors to know that my experience is far from unique. So, no, I wasn't shocked that people liked the book!

MMM: When you were writing *Benjamin's Parasite* did you ever feel like a parasite was crawling around in your gut causing intestinal mayhem? Or an itching feeling that insects were crawling all over your skin at night? Or is it just me?

STRAND: It's just you. Your susceptibility has been noted. Honestly, I'm not a writer who scares himself, creeps himself out, makes himself laugh, makes himself cry, or makes himself paranoid that nightmarish parasites are squirming around in his intestinal tract. I wanted my fire ant novel *Mandibles* to be as creepy/crawly/itchy as possible, but I didn't feel like fire ants were scurrying up my pant leg while I was writing it.

MMM: You have emceed the Bram Stoker Award ten times. What were some of your high moments and low moments of hosting the award ceremonies?

STRAND: My favorite single moment was successfully incorporating a jump scare into one of the introductions. Another high point was presenting the award named after Richard Laymon with Richard Laymon's actual ashes resting on the podium. (They were in a container; it wasn't just a pile of them. That would have been tactless.) By Sunday morning, nobody cares anymore who emceed—they care about the winners!—but the Saturday night afterparty was always a lot of fun. Without actually going back through ten years' worth of notes, I think my single favorite joke was: "Why are we only hearing speeches from the winners tonight, when what the losers would say is much more interesting?"

There weren't many low points. There was the occasional joke that I thought would get a huge laugh that didn't quite land, and it can be frustrating to put so much work into the event and then read some internet troll saying, "Dude! It's Emceeing 101 that you don't leave the podium unattended!" My least favorite year was when a couple of big Horror Writers Association controversies exploded right before the awards, and I didn't think I could get away with not addressing them. I got some good jokes out of it, but it was a particularly nerve-wracking year. I guess the other low moment goes back to "by Sunday morning, nobody cares anymore who emceed." But overall, there were way more highs than lows, or I wouldn't have done it for a decade!

MMM: *Clowns Vs. Spiders* has clowns and giant spiders in it. What are some of your favorite giant spider movies?

STRAND: Hopefully I'll be able to cheat and say *Clowns Vs. Spiders: The Movie* someday. It could happen. Stuff is in development. My favorite spider movie is *Kingdom of the Spiders,* but those are regular-sized spiders in large quantities, so I guess that's not the right answer. *Eight-Legged Freaks* loses points for the cartoony sounds the spiders make. I'll go with the '50s flick *Tarantula!*, because it earns the exclamation point in its title.

MMM: In the horror comedy (or is it comedy horror) book market your contemporaries (or competition) include Christopher Moore, David Wong, Max Brooks, Grady Hendrix, JA Konrath, James Moore, Michael A. Arnzen, the late, great Richard Laymon, and Michael McCarty (hey, how did that last one get in there)? Are you a fan of any of these gentlemen's works and are there any others we should include in this list?

STRAND: I'm a fan of all of them, although I'm not quite sure how James Moore got in there. Who associates the name "James Moore" with horror/comedy? I co-wrote *The Haunted Forest Tour* with him, and he was all like "Jeff! I wrote a joke in this chapter! A real joke! Aren't you proud of me?" I think you probably read *The Haunted Forest Tour* and gave us equal credit for the humor, even though Jim focused more on the disembowelments. But, yes, I like them all, including that McCarty scoundrel.

MMM: When writing horror comedy, how do you keep the book from being too horrific or too funny? What is a good way to balance the two elements out?

STRAND: I've never tried to keep a book from being too horrific, and it's never about being "too funny," but rather being *inappropriately* funny. Though there's a lot of humor in *My Pretties,* the novel is supposed to take place in the real world, with characters who react believably to the situation they're in. If I violated that for the sake of a joke, I'd be doing my job poorly. Meanwhile, *Cemetery Closing (Everything Must Go)* fits into the tradition of characters who wisecrack in the face of danger, so Andrew Mayhem is quite a bit wittier than I would be if I had a roaring chainsaw coming at me. That series takes place in a much more stylized world. Something like *Clowns Vs. Spiders* is an all-out horror/comedy, but I wanted both elements to work. If you don't think it's funny, hopefully it's still a great horror novel, and if you don't think it's scary, hopefully you still get a lot of laughs out of it. With each new book, I basically just establish the tone early on and try to stick to it.

MMM: How do you maintain an active fascination for horror?

STRAND: Read good books and watch good movies!

MMM: If you could be a monster, which monster would you be and why?

STRAND: A vampire who doesn't fit the traditional mythos, so he's got immortality and can turn into a bat, but he doesn't have to suck blood and won't disintegrate in the sunlight and can eat all the garlic he wants and see his reflection in a mirror and stuff. And he has normal teeth. The pale complexion is fine. Basically, a vampire with immortality but none of the standard weaknesses. Why do you ask? Can you make it happen?

MMM: What is the best advice another writer has ever given you?

STRAND: Brian Keene once shared his technique on how to get out of signing breasts when the request is made while you're in a committed relationship. I soaked up his valuable wisdom and eagerly awaited my opportunity to use it, but apparently Brian Keene is asked to sign breasts more frequently than I because I have yet to use his wisdom even once. But it's good to know that if the situation were ever to arise, I could successfully get out of signing breasts without any hurt feelings.

MMM: Of all the books you've written, which one was the easiest to write and which one the most difficult to write?

STRAND: The easiest was *A Bad Day for Voodoo*. The book was so ridiculous and so much fun to write. When I'm working on something that's filled with absurd storytelling elements (fake reviews at the beginning, a chapter that serves as its own book report, etc.) I'm totally in my element.

The hardest was probably *Stranger Things Have Happened*, a big wacky comedy written right after my dad died.

MMM: Why do you think young readers like your work with your Young Adult fiction? Do you think you still have a youthful spark in your heart?

STRAND: I'm certainly not old and crotchety, but I'm not sure I'd consider myself young at heart. I do think I'm good at tapping into the same kind of goofy humor that I enjoyed as a twelve-year-old. I don't mean fart jokes, but the shameless silliness I'd find in something like *Bananas* magazine. Though I'm not trying to learn their slang or write about modern video games, I think the tone of what I'd call "intelligent goofiness" is something that works for a twelve-year-old even when it's being written by a middle-aged dude.

MMM: What was the inspiration for *Cold Dead Hands*?

STRAND: Cemetery Dance asked me to write something for their novella series, and I was in the mood to write a chamber piece. So, after brainstorming various possible locations, I settled on "grocery store freezer." And I'd thought about a particularly ridiculous comment on the "guns don't kill people—people kill people" argument about how the Sandy Hook shootings could just as easily have been committed with a hammer. So, I came up with the idea of some gun nuts who want to prove their point by carrying out a full massacre without using guns, but it doesn't go well.

I tried to plot it in such a way that big events happened sooner than the reader might expect. "Wait—I thought this was going to be the finale! *Now* what's going to happen?"

MMM: Last words?

STRAND: "Hold my beer."

"My whole life is what it is basically because of science fiction. I have a degree in Byzantine history I wouldn't have if I hadn't read Lest Darkness Fall *(by L. Sprague de Camp) when I was fourteen years old."*
—Harry Turtledove

THE GUNS OF THE SOUTH
HARRY TURTLEDOVE

BY Cristopher DeRose & Michael McCarty

HARRY TURTLEDOVE BEGAN his career as a writer chronicling the Byzantine Empire and has since become one of the most prolific writers of Science Fiction, and arguably the leading voice of the sub-genre of alternate history. Harry began writing fiction under the pen name Eric G. Iverson with the novel *Wereblood* (1979). He continued under this pseudonym until 1985 when he also began writing under his own name, as well.

He was awarded the Hugo for his novella, "Down in The Bottomlands" in 1994 and soon became a bestseller in novel-length work with *The Guns of The South,* which would go on to win the John Esthen Cook Award for Southern Fiction. He has also won the Prometheus Award and the Sidewise Award.

Turtledove's other works are impressive, the numerous books include *Agent of Byzantium, Beyond the Gap, In the*

Presence of Mine Enemies, Opening Atlantis, Gunpowder Empire, Bombs Away, After the Downfall, Alpha and Omega Conan of Venarium an authorized prequel to Robert E. Howard's *Conan The Barbarian,* and many more.

Besides his considerable talent as a novelist and short story author, he has proven to be an accomplished collaborator as well working with S.M. Stirling on *Worlds That Weren't,* and *Household Gods* with Judith Tarr, as well as actor Richard Dreyfuss with *The Two Georges.*

Harry is married to mystery author Laura Frankos and has three daughters. His website can be found at: www.sfsite.com/~silverag/turtledove.html

MORE MODERN MYTHMAKERS: Is there any historical figure you haven't written about yet, that you'd like to?

HARRY TURTLEDOVE: Oh sure, there are lots of them. I don't like to name names, just yet, because when I talk about stuff before I write it—it has a tendency to go out of my head before I do it (laughs).

MMM: In *Rule Britannia,* in which you have William Shakespeare as a main character, you write Shakespearean poetry and plays in the book. Was this hard to do? Have you had any feedback from Shakespearean scholars on the accuracy of the prose?

TURTLEDOVE: This was probably the scariest thing I have ever tried because one of the worst things for a writer to do is write about a writer who is better than he is. Shakespeare is better than everybody. What I did was, adopt and adapt real Shakespearean lines as much as I could, use work by his contemporaries who sound more like him than I do, fill in the blanks, and make some of the bad puns myself (laughs).

So far, I haven't had any feedback yet. I haven't seen any of that. The reviews have been good though.

MMM: On the same line, what sort of preparation did you do for *Rule Britannia*? Why do you think that Shakespeare is still so popular after almost five centuries?

TURTLEDOVE: I got the idea in 1995. I immediately did what I always do. I started buying a bunch of books about the period. Those sent me in other directions, which sent me into buying other books. So, I read, read and read. I was in London, and I went to the New Globe Theater, and I went to the Tower (of London). Reading and seeing the sites are the best things you can do (laughs).

The reason for Shakespeare's popularity is because there is no one in the English language who has written better, ever, or who has ever come close.

MMM: What inspired you to include Spanish playwright Lope de Vega in *Rule Britannia*?

TURTLEDOVE: I needed someone on the Spanish side, who would be trying to stop what Shakespeare was up to. In real history, Lope de Vega did sail in the Armada, he was one of the few, who were lucky enough to come to Spain. It was reasonable to assume he would have stayed in England as an occupier if the Armada had won. He was a playwright himself. So, he might find himself involved in the English theater. He was someone who had an active time with women all through his life, which made him an interesting character to write in that regard. You put that all together and he seemed like the ideal foil for Shakespeare.

MMM: How do you still maintain an active fascination for science fiction?

TURTLEDOVE: My whole life is what it is basically because of science fiction. I have a degree in Byzantine history I wouldn't have if I hadn't read *Lest Darkness Fall* (by L. Sprague de Camp) when I was fourteen years old. Because I have that degree and the research skills that went with it, which set up most of what I have written. I would have probably written something else if I had done something different with my academic background because I already had the bug. This influenced what I had done. I met my wife when I was teaching history at UCLA.

If it weren't for science fiction, I wouldn't have the degree I have, I wouldn't have written most of what I have written, I wouldn't be married to the lady whom I am married to, I wouldn't have the kids I have. Other than that, it hasn't changed my life at all (laughs).

MMM: Alternate history has been a sub-genre in science fiction for a very long time. You mentioned *Lest Darkness Fall* (1939) in which L. Sprague de Camp's hero is thrown back to sixth-century Italy and has a chance to remake history. What are some of your favorite alternate history science fiction novels?

TURTLEDOVE: Obviously *Lest Darkness Fall* is one of them. H. Beam Piper's *Lord Kalvan of Otherwhen*, Poul Anderson's time-travel stories are classics—I grew up on those. Kim Newman and S.M. Stirling also does good work.

Two who I have been particularly impressed with this year are Kim Stanley Robinson's *Years of Rice and Salt,* and Steve Barne's *Lion's Blood*.

There are lots of people doing good work out there.

MMM: Why do you think your books became so popular in the alternate history genre?

TURTLEDOVE: I like to think that they are classics of Western literature (laughs). More realistically, I think it is partially because I do have a background in history. I'm lucky to make other times and other places seem real. I'm able to extrapolate from what did happen here and there, to what might have happened if things had gone differently.

MMM: Why do you think science fiction and history go together so well?

TURTLEDOVE: I think what alternate history does is the same sort of thing that other science fiction does. Other science fiction will change the present or near future, and will look at the farther future and see the effects of the change.

What alternate history does is change the more distant pasts and look at the more recent past. You extrapolate the same kind of way. You do it back in time instead of forward in time.

They are sort of Siamese twins.

MMM: Just different ends of the spectrum? The past instead of the future?

TURTLEDOVE: Exactly.

MMM: Why did you write *Wereblood* and *Werenight* under a pseudonym?

TURTLEDOVE: My publisher gave me that pseudonym on the grounds that no one would believe that Turtledove (which is my real name) was my real name. I had no choice in the matter.

I was just starting to be known under my pseudonym of Eric Iverson. I kept the pen name for a while. I was also publishing academic non-fiction. I thought it might be useful to have one name for fiction and one name for non-fiction.

When I sold the four books of the *Videssos Cycle* to

Lester del Rey (of Del Rey Books), Lester said, "I'm going to give you your real name back, because people will remember it."

I may be the only writer around who has both his pen name and his own name opposed to him by force (laughs).

MMM: You wrote *The Two Georges* with Richard Dreyfuss. How was it working with Richard Dreyfuss? And because of the Dreyfuss connection, has Hollywood sparked an interest in that book?

TURTLEDOVE: *The Two Georges* has been optioned (to be made into a movie). I have no idea if it will be produced.

It was fascinating working with Dreyfuss. I got to see him reading my dialogue aloud and listening to him. This was extremely instructive of what works and what does not work when you hear a trained actor delivering your lines. I learned a lot; I enjoyed it a lot.

MMM: Do you have any concern about being pigeonholed as an alternate history writer? Is there other science fiction you'd like to write?

TURTLEDOVE: I write all kinds of things. I write historical fantasy. I write funny fantasy. I write hard SF. I write straight historical fiction under another name.

If you do the same thing over and over again, you might as well drive a truck for heaven's sake.

MMM: Token history question. In history class, we're taught that America won the War of 1812. However, The British set fire to the White House, and the U.S. Capitol in the battle we won. The Battle of New Orleans was fought after the war was over. Did we really win the War of 1812, or was it more of a diplomatic victory?

TURTLEDOVE: The War of 1812 was essentially a push; we puff it up because no country likes to admit that they lost (laughs) or came out even.

MMM: You've edited a number of alternate history anthologies. What are the most common mistakes writers make when writing alternate science fiction stories?

TURTLEDOVE: Most of the common mistakes come with any writing that isn't so good—bad characters, bad plots, bad writing. The ones, which are peculiar to alternate histories, are bad research and bad extrapolation.

MMM: Last words?

TURTLEDOVE: I'd like to close with the same thing any writer automatically thinks when he is talking to his readers, "Buy my books please. I know you'd like them." (Laughs).

"As for Steve (King's) 'Popsy,' we'd met when the first Masques *debuted at the '84 World Fantasy Convention and, in my opinion, he wished he'd been in it. So, he sent 'Popsy' to me via agent Kirby McCauley, I made a few phone calls, and* Masques II *was quickly born."*

—J.N. Williamson

DON'T TAKE AWAY THE LIGHT
J.N. WILLIAMSON

GERALD **"JERRY" NEAL WILLIAMSON** was a horror writer and editor known under the name J. N. Williamson. Born in Indianapolis, Indiana, he studied journalism at Butler University, in the same city. He published his first novel in 1979, and went on to publish more than 40 novels and 150 short stories, averaging 2.69 books per year.

In 2003, he received a lifetime achievement award from the *Horror Writers Association.* He edited the critically acclaimed *How to Write Tales of Horror, Fantasy & Science Fiction* which covered the themes of such writing, and cited the work of many writers including Robert Bloch, Richard Matheson. Ray Bradbury, William F. Nolan and Stephen King.

Williamson edited the popular anthology series, *Masques* (also published as *Dark Masques*). His novels included *The Offspring, Don't Take Away the Light, The Evil One, Spree, Babel's Children, The Night Seasons, The Ritual, Dead to the World,* and *Affinity.*

Often regarded by his peers and colleagues as the grandmaster of horror. A newspaper once called him "the Lord of Gore."

J.N. Williamson passed away on December 8, 2005.

MORE MODERN MYTHMAKERS: Have you ever based any of your stories, in whole or in part, on a nightmare?

J.N. WILLIAMSON: It's possible I would never have written a novel if I hadn't dreamt the entire plot, including the primary characters' names, to *The Offspring*. That was back in the mid-70's. I began jotting the whole thing down the next day, amazed by the detail. My outline wound up running nearly 30,000 words. While *Offspring* didn't sell at once—it was my twenty-first novel—it got me an agent (the late Ray Puechner). Later I found I could summon plots at will. I wrote about it in the Mort Castle-edited books, *Writing Horror* and *On Writing Horror* .

MMM: When did you start writing?

WILLIAMSON: Apparently the first thing I wrote was a seven-year-old's tribute to my beloved grandma. She lived with us for most of my growing-up years, and the piece I wrote about her, now in a scrapbook, was published in one of our daily newspapers.

My first fiction probably was a Sherlock Holmes pastiche, "The Terrible Death of Crosby, The Banker," which I imprudently accepted for the first of *Illustrious Client's Case-Books* which I co-edited for the world of Baker Street Irregulars. The books were fine and are now quite rare, but I was fourteen years old. I'd like to think my writing has improved since then.

MMM: Many writers have shunned the term "horror writer." How does the term fare with you?

WILLIAMSON: I don't publish things I'm ashamed of. It's a fact that I'm a much-published writer who is best known for horror and supernatural fiction.

But a publisher—a commercial house—plans to make me an offer soon for a story collection, and its working title, *Frights Of Fancy*, says a lot about the approach I take to writing. The tales I'm choosing to reprint are from all over the commercial and small presses and reflect dozens of shades of mood and style of not just horror, but occult horror, crime horror, psychological horror, end-of-the-world horror, whimsically classic horror, erotic horror—plus dark fantasy, and a Sherlock Holmes pastiche!

I think life is often full of frightening challenges and that, frequently, people's beliefs add to the mysterious nature of what we confront, and either assist us in finding solutions, or can lead to our destruction.

MMM: You have written over 40 books and hundreds of short stories—all on a typewriter. Any plans of getting a word processor or a computer?

WILLIAMSON: No, no plans of that kind. I couldn't afford the time to learn how to use a new kind of machinery. I'd rather write, sell it, and have it appear in print.

MMM: What was the inspiration for *Don't Take Away the Light*? And was it difficult to write such an autobiographical novel?

WILLIAMSON: Somewhere F. Scott Fitzgerald claimed a good writer should be able to report accurately on his own funeral, and that cool idea caused me to think of writing in novel form about my own boyhood. It proved so difficult that I spent seven or eight years trying to get *Don't Take Away the Light* right.

I never had any inclination to attack "Dear," my mother, who was the most talented woman I've ever known. And in real life, she didn't do all the terrible things to me that happen to Teddy, the fictionalized version of me.

Also, I didn't have an imaginary playmate. But the rest of it—the phantom callers, the enemas, the destruction of my comics and comic rack and the alcoholism in the family—was as real as Dear's incredible musical talent.

MMM: How did you get Stephen King to write a short story for your *Masques* anthology?

WILLIAMSON: I'd love to edit *Masques* V—and *Masques* IX and X and XXI! Publishers with any interest, please step forward! As for Steve's "Popsy," we'd met when the first *Masques* debuted at the '84 World Fantasy Convention and, in my opinion, he wished he'd been in it. So he sent "Popsy" to me via agent Kirby McCauley, I made a few phone calls, and *Masques* II was quickly born.

MMM: *Spree* is a fast-paced action novel that would make an excellent movie. Do you have any plans on turning it into a screenplay?

WILLIAMSON: I've written only one screenplay, because I thought it might attract interest and make a suspenseful horror movie. It was accepted by an agent at a major film agency. The novel I based it on was *The Night Seasons*. The agent left to go it alone and I never heard from him again or even got my script back. I had no further interest in suffering with reckless no-talents on the West Coast just as I've been suffering so long with their agents and publisher brethren on the other coast.

I appreciate your compliment, but the way I see it now is that if God decides I'm supposed to make a lot of money from Hollywood, fine, I have as many graphic or visual novels that would work effectively as the other nice guy, Dean Koontz, who also had to wait an absurd length of time for the "Left Coast" to recognize his potential. Seventeen of my novels would be filmed in a fair, logical and book-reading world, and all but two or three could be done on reasonable budgets. However, they still exist as novels and, if they were filmed, the same thing would be true! The only important distinction would be the money.

MMM: You were with the Horror Writers Association at the beginning. What was the HWA like in the early days? And are you surprised by how big it has become?

WILLIAMSON: There was a great deal of excitement, numerous differences of opinion, and a certain optimism that all of us would manage the kind of apparent overnight success Steve King did.

I was inundated with work, since I was elected as the only combined secretary and treasurer the HWA would ever have, and I had to go on being a full-time writer. Dean Koontz served as a president and made all the tough, early decisions, or we submitted them for a vote. He and I vowed we'd never accept such offices again. But in review, I enjoyed persuading writers to join, among them Ray Bradbury and Harlan Ellison.

I'm not really surprised because I believe Dean, Paul Dale Anderson, and I laid the proper foundation for growth, along with certain other people.

MMM: Talking about Dean Koontz—was he the inspiration for the character Dean Knight in *The Monastery*?

WILLIAMSON: No, it wasn't in any way borrowed from Dean. But I always try to find interesting names for major characters, so I decided to use his first name. I chose the family name "Knight" because I'm a great fan of Indiana

University Head Basketball Coach Bob Knight. As a matter of fact, I've often mentioned him and players of his, including the wonderful now-retired guard Isiah Thomas, who guides the fortunes today of the Toronto Raptors.

Many times I've combed box scores of many teams to find interesting names. I had a protagonist named Westphal and a minor character called Hazlik. Each was a fine NBA player, then coach.

MMM: Are there times when you managed to scare yourself with what you write?

WILLIAMSON: At some level, probably every time out. This was particularly true for the first four novels or so, maybe because you run up so much higher a body count in a horror novel than in most short fiction. I think it's more likely because I was an imaginative new novelist and I was surprised to find all these gore-making machines in my mind, like $39 wonders advertised on little independent TV channels on Saturday nights, late.

Two or more times I even made lists of ascending horrific events—each one scarier than the last—and plotted novels around them.

But the lastingly frightening moments are connected to characters the readers like, surprise, nearly baffling problems and challenges, and bizarre other-worldly events entirely beyond the protagonist's life experience.

MMM: Last question—in *Premonition*, you featured a scene with a dinosaur in an amusement park long before the movies *Jurassic Park* and *The Lost World: Jurassic Park* were made. Does this give you a smidgen of satisfaction?

WILLIAMSON: What would give me such satisfaction would be knowing there is a parallel world in which (Michael) Crichton's wonderful idea for a novel occurred to a truly gifted writer who then crafted the fabulous adventure thriller *Jurassic Park* could have become.

I felt like crying while I read that pot-boiler.

I had forgotten I set *Premonition* on an island that had featured an amusement park. What I hadn't forgotten was creating, from researched myth—a literal sex object, capable of seducing anyone, whose embrace gave man or woman advanced cancer! The Alouqua may be the most clever monster in my fiction, and she appeared in a yarn with a pterodactyl and one of the early uses of cloning in any modern novel. I think readers got their money's worth with that old book (laughs).

"I love science fiction. I think it is more necessary than ever. We're living in a time right now, when all sorts of things are happening which/that are totally new and different and very troubling."

—Connie Willis

UNCHARTED TERRITORY
CONNIE WILLIS

BY CRISTOPHER DEROSE & MICHAEL MCCARTY

CONNIE WILLIS BEGAN her career as an author the old-fashioned way, as a certain saying goes; she earned it. Going from relative unknown to name author and winning a plethora of awards and honors as well.ell.

A multiple awards speculative author, she has won 11 Hugos, 7 Nebulas (Willis is the first person to win Nebulas in all four categories of fiction: novel, novella, novelette, and short story), the John W. Campbell Award, and the Damon Knight Memorial Grand Master Lifetime Achievement Award.

As a novelist, she was able to tell tales of the most serious of narratives, then turn out wisecracks while allowing the reader to be provoked into thought, never once speaking down to them. Connie takes us on speculator sojourners through the speculative fiction road with edgy alternate histories, "what ifs," science fiction stories, and even into death itself.

Her works include the novels *Water Witch* with Cynthia Felice, *Lincoln's Dreams*, *Light Raid* with Cynthia Felice, *Doomsday Book*, *Remake*, *Uncharted Territory*, *Bellwether*, *Promised Land* with Cynthia Felice, *Say Nothing of the Dog*, *Passage*, *Blackout* and *All Clear*.

Her novellas include *Daisy in The Sun*, *Inside Job*, *D.A.*, *All Seated on the Ground*, *All About Emily*, *I Met a Traveler in an Antique Land*, *Jack,* and *Take a Look at the Five and Dime*.

Her short story collections *Fire Watch*, *Impossible Things*, *Futures Imperfect*, *Miracle and Other Christmas Stories*, *Winds of Marble Arch and Other Stories*, *The Best of Connie Willis*, *A Lot Like Christmas*, *Terra Incognita,* and a nonfiction chapbook called *Roswell, Vegas, and Area 51: Travels with Courtney.*

In a world where pigeonholing has become the norm, Connie Willis has done well to evade such a thing. Equally humorous, thought-provoking, and/or, utterly serious in whatever world she decides to create and walk around in, Willis' work is known for running the gamut of emotional response as she effortlessly turns her own brand of mirror upon us and allows us to conceive of the answer ourselves while supplying her own.

She refuses to back down from the very concept of what awaits us past the brink of death, or to show translucently what we all can become, and often are. Willis is methodical in her research but knows not to overwhelm her readers with how much she has learned about a given topic. Instead, she makes sure she understands it well enough to tell the tale she wishes to tell.

While perhaps known for her more historical fiction, Willis has proven herself comfortable in whichever kind of speculative fiction she chooses to write, spotting her stories' likable characters (or, if unlikeable, at least in the realm of the interesting) and letting the reader wade their way in instead of being qualified at the door. With over ten compelling novels and collections and counting, she must be doing something right.

MORE MODERN MYTHMAKERS: Do the things that motivated you to write in the first place continue to drive you today?

CONNIE WILLIS: There's a scene in a Fred Astaire movie (how appropriate!), in which Ginger Rogers comes up to complain that Fred's dancing in the room above her is keeping her awake, and he leans against the door and grins at her and says, "Sometimes I just find myself dancing," and she says, "I suppose it's an affliction." That's how I think of my writing—as an affliction rather than a career choice. I have always wanted to write, never thought I would actually be able to sell anything, but had to do it, in spite of the fact that the actual job—contracts, correspondence, business deals, deadlines—drives me absolutely nuts. It cheered me up to read recently that it drove Agatha Christie crazy, too. But, no, I guess my motivation compulsion hasn't changed at all.

MMM: Did you come away with a different opinion about death and what may or may not wait for us on the other side after you completed *Passage*?

WILLIS: I have always thought a lot about death and what, if anything, might happen afterwards. Most of the time those thoughts have been forced on me by terrible things like the loss of loved ones or threats of illness, so it was actually kind of fun to have an excuse to think about death and its implications all day long for several years in an impersonal and logical way. Well, semi-logical. There's no way to be completely detached when it comes to death. As to what I believe about it, I don't know if that's changed or not. Whenever I try to think about possible after-existences,

I always come up smack against the cold equations of brain death—and I have absolutely no interest in any survival of molecules or life forces or whatever—if I'm not there in some recognizable way, what good would it be?

On the other hand, I believe very strongly that the people who have loved us (and sometimes, unfortunately, the other ones) are with us every day, surviving in our hearts and our feelings and our actions, affecting everything, which is certainly a form of immortality, and I definitely believe that "just because you want something to be true, doesn't mean it isn't." Mostly, though, I believe what Thornton Wilder said at the end of *The Bridge of San Luis Rey*: "There is a land of the living and a land of the dead and the bridge is love, the only survival, the only meaning."

MMM: Did all the awards and critical acclaim that *Passage* received surprise you? When you were going out promoting the book across the country, did you find that the American public did or did not want to talk about death?

WILLIS: The answer is yes to both (laughs). There are a lot of people who are very troubled by the whole idea of death, they would rather not think about it—ever. It's almost a kind of magic thinking. It's like when you say, "Gee, I hope my plane doesn't crash." And people say, "Don't even say that." As if saying it, is bringing it about. I think it is a very troubling topic to a lot of people.

On the other hand, this is something that affects everybody—

especially right now. I wrote the book before 9/11, and it came out before 9/11, and that makes people even more aware of sudden, terrifying death. The whole Boomer generation is reaching the point where they are dealing with this with their parents and having friends die. They are being brought face-to-face with the issue, if they want to be or not.

I think there is a need to talk about it. In our society, people don't talk about it much. They'll talk about it a little at the funeral, they tend to say a number of platitudes and that's it. If you do have a conversation about death, people will say, "that's really morbid." And try to change the subject.

I welcomed the chance to write the book, there were people who needed and wanted to talk about the subject and don't have a lot of outlets. I thought it was a good sign that the non-fiction book *How We Die* (by Sherwin Nuland) was a bestseller on the New York Times Bestseller list. There are the near-death experience books, which basically say, "Don't worry, big hugs on the other side. Death is nothing. It will be fun." Then there are the various religious takes on death, their particular view of what the afterlife is like. But nobody was talking about death in general.

People will come up and talk to me and say, "my mom died after a long illness and I read *Passage* when she was sick." And I'm thinking "Oh no. I didn't want to add to your misery." And they'll say, "It's the perfect book, because I'm already thinking about those kinds of things. This book gave me the opportunity to look at that."

I think people are closest interested in death, they are afraid to come out and say they are interested in that.

MMM: Let's talk about the *Black Out* and *All Clear* novels. What does "all clear" mean?

WILLIS: All clear's meaning is after the siren, meaning the raid was over, when it was safe to come out of the shelters during the Blitz in London during World War II.

I was working on a novel about aliens and Roswell that went smash on September 11th (2001), along with so many other things. It's just not the right plot, the right time, and the right tone for that book. I abandoned it for the time being. I'll come back to some of the same themes later.

I decided to write some of the things we were going through and our circumstances; now, we have a lot in common with the London Blitz. Especially the uncertainty of what is going to happen next—living from day to day not knowing what the next blow is. Not seeing our way clear.

One of my themes in my time travel novels (*Fire Watch* and *Doomsday Book*) is how time travelers—although they try very hard to put themselves into the place of the people living through that time, they really can't because they know how it turns out.

Even if you went back and experienced the Blitz, and bombs were falling above your head, you were going through many of the same emotions. At the same time, you wouldn't be because you know Hitler didn't invade. You know he didn't use poisonous gas. You know that the Allies eventually triumphed. You also know some of the terrible things that happened, they don't—like the Holocaust. Basically, it is a huge advantage to know that it's all going to work out.

The basic story, I have several people working the Blitz, working various parts of World War II in England. One of them is with the evacuated children in the countryside, another is there during the phony war before the bombs actually fall, and one is actually working the Blitz. One's working with a fake army in Kent, where they were trying to convince Hitler that we were going to invade across Calais instead of Normandy.

Suddenly, they find themselves stranded and they have no idea why. They have no idea what is going on in their future. Don't know if something has malfunctioned in the time travel itself, or in fact, or their present life has been attacked in some way, or war has broken out, or a meteor has destroyed the whole world and they don't know what, and they can't get back.

Although they are there together, in the sense that they are all in the past, they are not in the same place and they are not at the same time.

They're coping with much of the same uncertainty as those in the Blitz.

It may sound grim, but it actually has a lot of humor in it. The evacuated children story is very funny in many ways.

World War II is especially an interesting time because there were parts of it that were absolutely fascinating and exciting and other parts that were terrible and tragic and other parts that were very funny.

MMM: When do you decide to use the element of humor in your work? Before or after you have the plot and characters in place?

WILLIS: That is such a tough question. Basically, humor is my natural state. It is how I see the world. If I'm dealing with a serious story, I try to keep the humor from coming in. When I'm working with serious work, I'm using irony, which is the dark side of humor. I guess it is never totally absent.

I feel if you are writing a book-length work, you better have some humor in it somewhere. (William) Shakespeare put the porter scene in the middle of *Macbeth*, one of his grimmest plays. He knew that there needed to be some comic relief there.

One of the reasons I have always been attracted to the London Blitz, which I'm working on right now with *Blackout* and *All Clear*, is that there was so much humor in this terrible situation. The Blitz was very well documented to have had lots of humor. People would have had their shop windows blown out and they'd be sweeping up the glass and they'd put up a big sign that'd say, "Open For Business And We Do Mean *OPEN!*" Or "Special Hitler Half Price Sale." That is how they coped. That was their coping mechanism. There is a lot of comic potential even though this is a dark period of history.

MMM: Of all your novels, which one is your personal favorite?

WILLIS: My favorite story of all time that I have ever written is *Fire Watch*. I don't think it is my best story.

I was very much a beginning writer, when I wrote that one. And beginning writers flay around wildly. One time they'll almost get it perfect, the next time they are clear out in left field. They are like a wild pitcher. One time they'll strike someone else, the next they'll hit the backboard or the catcher (laughs). That's how I felt. I knew exactly what I wanted to do, I had them very clear in my head, but when it came down to putting it down on paper—oh my God—who knew if I was going to get anywhere close to it.

When we went to England for the first time, I wanted very much to go to St. Paul's because I had read about the fire watch and read how they slept down in the crypts during the day and came up to the roofs at night to look for bombs. I thought that was very romantic.

I had an idea I was going to write a kind of poem about the contrast between sleeping down there with the dead bodies of all those people who were killed in other battles and other times and facing their own war up above.

That is about as far as I had gotten.

Then we went to St. Paul's. I fell in love with it. I think it's the most beautiful place in the world. We went up in the dome, climbed up through the gallery and went outside. And I went outside, and I looked out, expecting to see— some kind of Mary Poppins landscape—chimney pots and things.

Instead, it is the ugliest landscape I have ever seen in my life. It is all concrete, Bauhaus glass block buildings, it is just hideous looking. It doesn't look like London at all. It looks like Cleveland or something.

I'm standing there thinking, this is a huge disappointment and then it hits me. Oh my God, the reason it looks like this is because everything here was built in the 1950s—because everything burned down.

When I realized that all four sides were burned, I thought—there's no way that this church survived. This cathedral could not have possibly survived the war.

Then I was truly fascinated. That day I said to my husband Courtney and our friends, "You guys will have to please go away for a while, I'm taking notes, I have to stand here and take notes. I have this brilliant idea."

I stood there for three hours taking notes on everything I thought I might need in a story and everything I could think of. Of course, I didn't have the notes I needed when I got back home.

When I got home, I did all this research on the fire watch, the Blitz, London, and everything. I just fell totally in love with the whole story. I actually was able to tell the story I wanted to tell in a way that I thought worked very well.

It's still my favorite story. I like when they give my stories an award, I think "Yeah that was one of my better stories," I'm always surprised at what gets attention and what doesn't.

MMM: *Firewatch, Blackout, All Clear,* and *Jack* all take place during the London Blitz. You've noted that this is your favorite historical time period. Why?

WILLIS: I keep writing about the Blitz. Plus, in *To Say Nothing of the Dog* there is a segment in Coventry during the Blitz. I kept writing about it, hoping I'd get it out of my system. I realized I needed to do an entire book about World War 2. I find the Blitz endlessly fascinating.

It was a time where the front comes to the people. It is kind of like 9/11 with that kind of drama and emotional intensity repeated night after night after night. The Blitz went on through the whole war sporadically. From

September 7th, 1940 through May 1941 there were nightly bombings. They had these devastating things happen to them, but didn't have a chance to recover. It was an ongoing barrage of terrible things happening. Over 60,000 civilians died in the Blitz.

The people managed to continue coping after these incredible circumstances. Getting to work in the morning was an ordeal. You'd be sleeping all night in a shelter, or you didn't get any sleep at all, then you would go back to your flat, to change clothes. Which may or may not be there. Even if it is there, it may or may not have any water or electricity because that may have been bombed in the night and they don't have it hooked up again. Then you have to struggle to get to work. The buses have all been rerouted, your normal method of getting to work is all out of whack, because there is a big double-decker bus, stuck in a big hole halfway down a tube station.

The tubes (subways) and the buses are both out. You have to walk around all these fallen things—just to get to work. Yet, everyone went to work every day.

The English are known for being quiet, reserved and not talking to strangers. They began talking to each other and saying, "good luck tonight," "hope I see you in the morning," to acknowledge this fear, that they might not live through the night; that any night could be the bomb with your name on it.

How do you live? When you have no idea what is going to happen tomorrow? That is one of the reasons I'm writing *All Clear*, because I'm fascinated by the whole time period of the Blitz. Although I wrote before about the tube stations and St. Paul's, the Blitz is huge, there are tons of stuff I haven't written about. I am also fully convinced that it was Britain's finest hour.

MMM: You use time travel in several of your works. How did you get interested in this topic?

WILLIS: The first time travel novel I read was Robert Heinlein's *A Door into Summer,* which is a great time travel novel. I just fell in love with the whole idea of time travel. I just think that it is so endlessly interesting. I'm not interested at all in the mechanics of time travel, how would you put together this time machine? How would it physically work? I'm interested in the theory of time travel. How do you deal with the paradoxes? How do you deal with the grandfather paradox? If you go back in time and you changed the future, and become part of that system, you changed the future, but if you changed the future, that future that you were once living in doesn't exist for you to come back from, it just gets endlessly complicated. It is what I call the theory of time travel and how it would work if we had such a thing.

Then the whole idea of the ethical dilemmas that time travel creates. Which time travel writers have been in love with forever! If you had a chance to go back and stop Hitler, by killing a completely innocent person, would you do that? Should you do that?

If you have this clear shot at Hitler, who clearly is a good person to shoot in 1933, should you shoot him? Everybody says, "Yes." But I don't know. If it meant that Germany would be sitting there and nursing its wounds for another 30 years and finally when another demi-god like Hitler rose, it would be during the time of The Bomb. I think that would be worse.

There are all kinds of scenarios you can come up with which are worse than what happened.

That makes time travel very interesting.

One of the things I'm doing with *Blackout* and *All Clear;* is what if you got trapped in time, in the past, how could you communicate with the future? How can you tell them how to come get you? Or how can you get out of it on your own. It is different from being stranded in Hong Kong, where you could get a cell phone and call somebody. This is being really stranded.

I love writing about time travel. I have two or three other time travel stories.

MMM: Did the inspiration for *Remake* come from a love of classic film or several ideas for a science fiction book that led to detailed research?

WILLIS: The inspiration for *Remake* came from lots of places—my boundless admiration for Fred Astaire who's my hero—he works so hard to make it all look so easy, which should be the goal of art, and he seems to have been a completely humble person, I suppose the result of working all those years with a sister who everyone said was the real talent of the group—and my love of movie musicals—you can probably tell which ones from the book. I actually had the idea (not quite in its finished form) years and years ago and kept lists of musical numbers that might work as I watched movies over the years. Unfortunately, I didn't get around to actually writing it until the computer graphics revolution was practically upon us—when I started the book, they'd just come out with that Coke commercial starring James Cagney and by the time I finished, *Toy Story* was coming out—and I had the problem of having the technology change constantly on me as I was writing the book and practically overtaking me, which it has done now. It actually seemed much more prophetic when it came out than it does to someone reading it now.

MMM: Collaborations have always been a staple in the sci-fi market—any other thoughts on the subject?

WILLIS: I'm happy to have the opportunity to answer the last question. Because a couple of people said, "When I saw you wrote with someone else, I just assumed it was one of the franchise things like the other authors have done."

Especially what the dead authors have done (laughs). When the name is on a book like Asimov's *Caves of Steel* series or some of the things Anne McCaffrey has done with other people, it's not really a collaboration at all.

But with us, these are true collaborations. We wrote alternating chapters, we brainstormed the plots together, we did the rewrites together, sat side by side going over the manuscripts, had some royal battles over different decisions in the books. True collaborations, I felt bad that anyone would think these were some kind of franchise—because that is a whole different kind of book.

I feel your name is a brand, but that you have an obligation when people see your name on a book, that you really wrote that book. I feel it cheapens everything. Not only is that work kind of a deception, but I feel it cheapens the previous work. The author only has his vision to offer. It is almost like false advertising in a way. I know it sounds really harsh, and science fiction has done it for years.

I hate the thought that someone would take my time travel characters after I was gone and done things with them I would have never approved of. Somehow diluted the work that I wrote by making it an endless 'adventures of...' I feel it hurts the whole thing, including the books that came before too. That's my rant for the day.

MMM: Do you sell a book from a proposal or from a finished manuscript?

WILLIS: *Lincoln's Dreams* and *Doomsday Book* I sold from a finished manuscript. Since then, I have done proposals. That means I'm always in trouble with my publishers because I'm very slow. People ask me why it took me five years to write *Doomsday Book*—it always takes me that long to write (laughs).

I was in so much trouble with *Passage*—I just didn't realize how long it would take—and they went ahead and scheduled it—not realizing that I couldn't be relied on (laughs).

Once it is scheduled and once it is in the catalog—it's sort of caught in the toils of a great machine. Where it doesn't matter that you're not done, it's getting published anyway. I hate that pressure.

I even have talked to my agent about going back to the original way of selling the completed manuscript. That would take some pressure off me.

I sure don't like working the way I have to work. I just can't tell how long things are going to take.

MMM: Why did you fashion *To Say Nothing of the Dog* after a Victorian novel?

WILLIS: Because I love Victorian novels. I thought I was the only person who did. Then I started talking to people when I was writing the book, and I discovered that there are many, many people who love Victorian novels. They like the style; they like the strange approach of using lots of characters and have lots of complications—where plot is supreme.

The second book I loved after I discovered science fiction was not science fiction. It was *Three Men in a Boat* by Jerome K. Jerome. The reason I read it second was because my first science fiction novel was *Have Spacesuit Will Travel* by Robert Heinlein. In that book, the very first chapter, the father won't talk to Kip because he's reading *Three Men in a Boat*, which he has read 1,000 times. So, I immediately went and found the book and read it, and it has always been one of my favorites. That novel was a complete self-indulgence because that is the book I would have wanted to read when I was a kid.

MMM: What advice would you give to beginning writers?

WILLIS: Write what you really care about. Don't ever write what you think the market is looking for, what you think people are interested in reading. Write for yourself.

I once read C.S. Lewis' essays. In it, he was talking about—you should write what you're interested in and not what you know.

The first thing Lewis ever said to (J.R.R.) Tolkien was "Have you ever seen a dragon?" and Tolkien said, "Yes," and Lewis said "Where?" and Tolkien said, "on Calvary."

Lewis went on to write that if dragons are what you are interested in, that is what you should write about. Heck if there is a market for dragons, or if people have written too much about dragons. Only write what you are really passionate about.

I always try to remind people that when Tolkien wrote *The Lord of the Rings*, there was no fantasy market. He had invented that market. People probably thought he was crazy for wasting his time writing about elves and dragons— things that only children cared about.

I think it is good career advice. I have never written any story for the money or have written any story because I thought it was what people wanted to read. I have written either to amuse myself, or it was something I passionately wanted to talk about.

MMM: Last words?

WILLIS: I love science fiction. I think it is more necessary than ever. We're living in a time right now when all sorts of things are happening that are totally new and different, and very troubling. In many ways, none of them are new at all, science fiction writers of the 1950s and 1940s have thought of a great many of these things.

One of the reasons we have a vocabulary to deal with the shift in personal liberties—the idea of how much security do you want? How many of those personal rights are you willing to trade for those securities—those go straight back to *1984* and *Brave New World*.

The fear of what can happen tomorrow. That someone can wipe us out. Those post-apocalypse stories have been around forever. I would recommend that people read the science fiction that is being written now, and see the science fiction of now at the movies; they should also be reading the classics.

It's always ironic to have the literature of the future, to read the classics (laughs). Science fiction is great to deal with all these current issues and crises. I'm glad to be in science fiction, to help give guidance to the future.

AFTERWORD

JEFFREY THOMAS

AS A WRITER in the genres of horror and science fiction (how else would I have become acquainted with the likes of Michael McCarty?), in a career dating back more than thirty years, I've been interviewed many times. So many times, that I've ended up being asked the same questions over and over again, in turn giving the same answers as if from a memorized script. Despite the fact that it's always flattering that anyone would want to interview me at all, I have to admit it can get tedious after a while. And so, let me tell you some reasons why I particularly value Michael McCarty as an interviewer.

For one thing, in books such as *Giants of the Genre* and *Masters of the Imagination*, and of course *Modern Mythmakers*, McCarty has not only interviewed a great many noted writers like Harlan Ellison, Richard Matheson, and Ray Bradbury (to literally name only a few), but directors like John Carpenter and Mick Garris, actors like Adrienne Barbeau, artists like Boris Vallejo, even the mentalist the Amazing Kreskin. So, as you can see, an interview book assembled by McCarty is going to be a varied and fascinating smorgasbord, not just a bunch of the same questions being asked of one group of people in the arts. And, as for those questions, I like the way McCarty goes about it. Yes, of course the expected questions must be asked ("Why do you write horror?") but he does his homework, he's familiar enough with his subjects that he knows the detailed questions to ask, the answers of which will prove more interesting, more unusual, for the effort the interviewer has put in.

And again, there are the sheer number of interview books McCarty has put together over the years. This tells you that there is a person who *loves* interviewing. He's not just doing the occasional piece for this publication or that website; it's a real passion for him, and passion's something that always comes across in one's endeavors.

Add to all this the fact that McCarty is a prolific writer of horror himself. He knows this stuff as an insider. Plus, he's a writer who frequently collaborates with other writers. This in itself demonstrates the fact that he understands how to get into another creative person's head, to learn their methodology.

Interviews with creative people are entertaining; they give us insights into the books and movies that we love. They allow us to better know our heroes, and introduce us to newer artists, or at least those we haven't been previously exposed to. And, for a writer like myself, getting into the minds of other creative types inspires me, because it would be a sad thing indeed if I didn't continue being inspired, learning, and growing.

If you've reached the end of this book, you already know what I'm talking about, don't you? You've already enjoyed, and profited from, the very things I describe.

And if you are a creative type, perhaps this book will even have taught you how to interview *yourself*, internally, so that you might dissect, contemplate, evolve, or celebrate your own process. If that's the case, let's thank Michael McCarty for putting us in that inquiring mindset. The guy really knows how to do this interview thing, doesn't he?

THE END?

Not if you want to dive into more of Crystal Lake Publishing's Tales from the Darkest Depths!

Check out our amazing website and online store.
https://www.crystallakepub.com

We always have great new projects and content on the website to dive into, as well as a newsletter, behind the scenes options, social media platforms, our own dark fiction shared-world series and our very own webstore. If you use the IGotMyCLPBook! coupon code in the store (at the checkout), you'll get a one-time-only 50% discount on your first eBook purchase!

Our webstore even has categories specifically for KU books, non-fiction, anthologies, more books by Michael McCarty, and of course more novels and novellas.

THE END

ABOUT THE AUTHOR

Michael McCarty has been a professional writer since 1983, and the author of over fifty books of fiction, including *I Kissed A Ghoul, Frankenstein's Mistress, Dark Cities: Dark Tales, A Little Help From My Fiends, Liquid Diet & Midnight Snack, Dark Duets, Dracula Transformed and Other Bloodthirsty Tales* (with Mark McLaughlin), *Lost Girl Of The Lake* (with Joe McKinney), the vampire *Bloodless* series: *Bloodless, Bloodlust* and *Bloodline* (with Jody LaGreca). He is a five-time Bram Stoker Finalist, and in 2008 won the David R. Collins' Literary Achievement Award from the Midwest Writing Center.

His nonfiction books include: *Esoteria-Land: The Authentic, Eclectic and Eccentric Nonfiction of Michael McCarty, Ghosts of the Quad Cities* (with Mark McLaughlin), *Eerie Quad Cities* (with John Brassard Jr.), and *Modern Mythmakers: 35 Interviews With Horror and Science Fiction Writers and Filmmakers* which features interviews with Ray Bradbury, Dean Koontz, John Carpenter, Richard Matheson, Elvira, Linnea Quigley, John Saul, Joe McKinney, and many more.

Michael McCarty lives in Rock Island, Illinois with his wife Cindy and pet rabbit Yeti.

Michael McCarty is on Twitter as michaelmccarty6. His blog site is at:

http://monstermikeyaauthor.wordpress.com

Facebook! Like him on his official page:

http://www.facebook.com/michaelmccarty.horror.

Crystal Lake Publishing's most popular non-fiction:

Readers . . .

Thank you for reading *More Modern Mythmakers*. We hope you enjoyed this non-fiction collection.

If you have a moment, please review *More Modern Mythmakers* at the store where you bought it.

Help other readers by telling them why you enjoyed this book. No need to write an in-depth discussion. Even a single sentence will be greatly appreciated. Reviews go a long way to helping a book sell, and is great for an author's career. It'll also help us to continue publishing quality books. You can also share a photo of yourself holding this book with the hashtag #IGotMyCLPBook!

Thank you again for taking the time to journey with Crystal Lake Publishing.

Visit our Linktree page for a list of our social media platforms. https://linktr.ee/CrystalLakePublishing

Our Mission Statement:

Since its founding in August 2012, Crystal Lake Publishing has quickly become one of the world's leading publishers of Dark Fiction and Horror books in print, eBook, and audio formats.

While we strive to present only the highest quality fiction and entertainment, we also endeavour to support authors along their writing journey. We offer our time and experience in non-fiction projects, as well as author mentoring and services, at competitive prices.

With several Bram Stoker Award wins and many other wins and nominations (including the HWA's Specialty Press Award), Crystal Lake Publishing puts integrity, honor, and respect at the forefront of our publishing operations.

We strive for each book and outreach program we spearhead to not only entertain and touch or comment on issues that affect our readers, but also to strengthen and support the Dark Fiction field and its authors.

Not only do we find and publish authors we believe are destined for greatness, but we strive to work with men and woman who endeavour to be decent human beings who care more for others than themselves, while still being hard working, driven, and passionate artists and storytellers.

Crystal Lake Publishing is and will always be a beacon of what passion and dedication, combined with overwhelming teamwork and respect, can accomplish. We endeavour to know each and every one of our readers, while building personal relationships with our authors, reviewers, bloggers, podcasters, bookstores, and libraries.

We will be as trustworthy, forthright, and transparent as any business can be, while also keeping most of the headaches away from our authors, since it's our job to solve the problems so they can stay in a creative mind. Which of course also means paying our authors.

We do not just publish books, we present to you worlds within your world, doors within your mind, from talented authors who sacrifice so much for a moment of your time.

There are some amazing small presses out there, and through collaboration and open forums we will continue to support other presses in the goal of helping authors and showing the world what quality small presses are capable of accomplishing. No one wins when a small press goes down, so we will always be there to support hardworking, legitimate presses and their authors. We don't see Crystal Lake as the best press out there, but we will always strive to be the best, strive to be the most interactive and grateful, and even blessed press around. No matter what happens over time, we will also take our mission very seriously while appreciating where we are and enjoying the journey.

What do we offer our authors that they can't do for themselves through self-publishing?

We are big supporters of self-publishing (especially hybrid publishing), if done with care, patience, and planning. However, not every author has the time or inclination to do market research, advertise, and set up book launch strategies. Although a lot of authors are successful in doing it all, strong small presses will always be there for the authors who just want to do what they do best: write.

What we offer is experience, industry knowledge, contacts and trust built up over years. And due to our strong brand and trusting fanbase, every Crystal Lake Publishing book comes with weight of respect. In time our fans begin to trust our judgment and will try a new author purely based on our support of said author.

With each launch we strive to fine-tune our approach, learn from our mistakes, and increase our reach. We continue to assure our authors that we're here for them and that we'll carry the weight of the launch and dealing with third parties while they focus on their strengths—be it writing, interviews, blogs, signings, etc.

We also offer several mentoring packages to authors that include knowledge and skills they can use in both traditional and self-publishing endeavours.

We look forward to launching many new careers.

This is what we believe in. What we stand for. This will be our legacy.

**Welcome to Crystal Lake Publishing—
Tales from the Darkest Depths.**